Behind the Wall

*A Story of Love,
Loss and Wonder*

Ginger Gilmour

Behind The Wall

NEW HAVEN PUBLISHING LTD
Published 2023
www.newhavenpublishingltd.com
newhavenpublishing@gmail.com

All Rights Reserved

The rights of Ginger Gilmour, as the author of this work, have been asserted in accordance with the Copyrights, Designs and Patents Act 1988.
No part of this book may be re-printed or reproduced or utilized in any form or by any electronic, mechanical or other means, now unknown or hereafter invented, including photocopying, and recording, or in any information storage or retrieval system, without the written permission of the Author and Publisher.

Cover Design © Ginger Gilmour

All photographs are courtesy of Ginger Gilmour's personal collection except for the photographs that have specific permission to be used. All sculptures and paintings are equally Ginger Gilmour's creative expressions as an artist.

Copyright © 2023 Ginger Gilmour
All rights reserved

ISBN: 978-1-912587-87-2

TIMELESS BEAUTY

Soul Expressing Strong And Free
Sacred Sounds Washing Over Me
As The Space Of Timeless Beauty
Where We All And Always Exist As One

Anger Turning Into Divine Power
For Release Allows Us All To See
That Anger At Its Core Is Beauty
When We Allow Our Self To Be

When We Truly Share Our Soul Expression
We All Know The Truth We Are Joined
As One Now And For Ever For Where We End
Is Where We Start

As The Space Of Timeless Beauty
Where We All And Always Exist As One
We Are All One For Ever Present Divine Love
Intending To Be True

As The Space
Where
We
Are All Free

(c) Andy Cooney 2002
You Tube Channel
https://www.youtube.com/@AndyCPaintsWords

Contents

Awakening 2023	7
It Was 28 October, Ann Arbor, Michigan 1971	10
Echoes Of Love - Arriving in NYC, 5 November 1971	20
Meeting The Parents - NYC, Carnegie Hall, 15 November 1971	22
Journey To England - November 5, 1971	25
Obscured By Clouds - Chateau D'Héreouville, France 1972	28
Dark Side Of The Moon Goes On The Road - Japan Tour 1972	30
Summer in Lindos, Rhodes, Greece, 1973	33
The Rose City, Marrakech - Gini Photo Shoot 1972, French Tour 1974	36
Kate Bush - Man With The Child In His Eyes 1973-1975	40
Gonna Get Married 7 July 1975	42
Paradise on Young Island, Caribbean 1976	49
Baby Alice Is Born - London, 8 MAY 1976	51
Early Childhood - Daddy hides us away, USA 1954	57
Animals In Flight - Battersea Power Station, December 1976	62
Pigs On The Road - European Tour 26–27 January 1977	65
The Bright Side Is Calling - Paris, France	67
Floyd Becomes Cecil Demille - Wembley Empire Pool 1977	70
Animal Farm Comes Stateside - In The Flesh Tour, U.S.A	73
Saving The Hogs - Oakland, California	77
Time Off In Paradise - Kauai, Hawaii, May–June 1977	79
Chicago, Chicago - Super Bowl, Soldier Field 19 JUNE 1977	83
A World Series Rock 'N' Roll Show - Cleveland, Ohio, 25 June 1977	85
A Reunion Of Family - Philadelphia, June 1977	89
A Parade Of Animals - New York City, 1-4 July 1977	92
Is There Anyone Listening? Montreal 6 JULY 1977	97
Time Out To Fly - David Gilmour Releases Solo Album 1977-1978	103
The Building Of The Wall - Financial Tragedy 1977-1980	105

Contents *Continued*

Tax Exile - Silent Beauty Disappears Behind The Wall 1979 108

Miracles Do Happen - Our Baby And Me Saved, 1978 115

Another Child Is Born - Clare, 1979 117

The Wall Comes Alive - Los Angeles 1980 121

New York, New York - February 1980 125

The Clash Of The Titans The Movie - THE WALL 127

Isn't She Lovely - Wall Concerts Earl's Court 1981 130

Sara Is Born At Home - Brockhurst Mansion, June 1981 132

"What Was That?" THE WALL Premieres, 1982 135

Searching For Humility - Soho, London 1983 138

Cecil Collins Classes, ILEA, London, 1983 140

Cecil Exhibition - Aldeburgh, Suffolk JUNE 1984 144

Guy Fawkes, Brockhurst 1984 147

Flying Again - ABOUT FACE 1984 150

ABOUT FACE Tour 1984 153

LIVE AID - We Can Feed The World, 1984 157

Another Child Is Born At Home - Matthew Gilmour, 1985 161

Momentary Lapse Of Reason - Daring To Be 1985–1989 165

Harmony Out Of Chaos - New York City 5–7 October 1987 169

Wembley Concert, August 1988 172

Daddy Too Loud - Japan 1988 174

David Leaves The Family - Where is Daddy? Comfortably Numb 176

House Of Broken Dreams - Kuaui, Hawaii 1989 180

Isle Of Dogs Concert, July 1989 183

Love, Loss & Wonder 185

AWAKENING
2023

As I sit by my window writing, a robin has appeared upon a branch while CNN's words of war and flooding capture my attention for a moment. Fortunately, I have come to realise that I am the robin, and we sing the same song of love, of oneness. It was not always that way. It has been a journey of self-discovery through many darkly lit alleyways. So many questions, so many doubts; what is life about? Who am I? I am no good. OH MY GOD! HELP ME! What am I supposed to do? Will I succeed? When will I find love?

Life was a drama of push and pull between pain and peace, desire and disappointments, between life and death while always trying to find balance and harmony. I was young, still a dreamer, just beginning to find my way, when in 1971 I met David Gilmour, and travelled with him on the Pink Floyd tour as he was the lead guitarist. Later, in 1975, we married. From that moment my life became an extraordinary adventure beyond anything I could have ever imagined.

For you, I am guided to share what I have discovered throughout all the challenges of such Love, Loss, and Beauty. Some may remember things differently. Some may find it too simple and sweet but in staying true to myself, my joy, my love, my pain, I mean no harm to anyone. I want to say, most of all, I have found something about life that I didn't know existed. It was the truth about the God within and its power to create peace.

Perhaps this is something you already know, or perhaps it is new to you, too. Perhaps you know that we are born with both the Dark and the Light within our being? And the struggles, the conflicts are there to push us into finding our Divinity within. I have come to know that we are, in the purity of our nature, powerful and magnificent, but we have no idea of this because most of us identify with the wrongs and not the rights; the fears, the anger instead of the love innate within our hearts. Most compare and compete, judge and disapprove even of themselves instead of touching the greatness of our potential and rejoicing in our differences.

My path of awakening took me through cycles of weakness and judgements within the rock 'n' roll world, especially after I chose to be a vegetarian, work with the healing power of colour, became aware of the guidance of angels and could finally say the word God. For a long time, I had my own devil on one shoulder taking me in one direction and an angel on the other. It took me years to choose and listen to the angel. Now I am so grateful for my choices that a smile warms my heart each day.

I remember all the concerts I was graced to have witnessed when we all shared in the Beauty of the music together. Time stood still as the notes floated over our heads and around the hall. There were so many moments when we were held in such stillness that our hearts were filled with Wonder and we held hands. I ask, "Do you ever feel loss because they no longer are together and play live?" Many do.

My journey has taken me through the doorway that was opened from their music and for a while was closed. I came to know that through art, music, dance and poetry there is a metaphysical power that transforms the chaos within our minds, within our hearts. Most of all this power lies innate in every one of us. I call to you to awaken to your inner Beauty. Know that what you felt in those concerts, or listening to music, or being touched by a film, or reading some poetry, is actually you opening your heart to know the Beauty of life. You opened the doorway! And you can be in that space every moment. It is ours when we choose.

I have come to know that there is such Beauty within and together for us to Live upon Earth only when we choose. It is beyond the spin, the drama, the chaos of our ordinary lives. This realisation is what I share with you within the pages of this book. It begins with the Love of a dream come true. It shares stories of our life within the challenges of Pink Floyd and beyond. It is my true story, and in the end it is my journey to have discovered 'Who I truly was born to BE!' beyond the backstage pass, beyond the idolatry, beyond the glamour, beyond the illusion.

I begin this story, telling of the events that changed my life forever. Enter lightly as you walk within my journey of Love and Awakening.

IT WAS 28 OCTOBER, ANN ARBOR, MICHIGAN 1971

I was living with Roger Pothus, a close friend, in a small mock Tudor house in Ann Arbor, Michigan. At first, we had a traditional relationship, which eventually became one of companionship. He was my best friend. Over the years, Roger took on the ownership and operations of two boutiques, one of which I managed. From our perspective, we were big fish in a little town, interacting with a population that liked the things that we offered in our clothing store. It was profitable and inspired creativity and individuality.

Ann Arbor was waking up after the deluge of the Vietnam War and the sixties movement had left its mark on the souls and taste of our clients. One day a dear friend of ours, Morpheus, returned from London. He had been living with us prior to his adventure across the ocean and had called our home his anchor. In addition to his stories, he brought back with him a taste of Carnaby Street with his snakeskin boots from Gohill's and his leopard skin-tight trousers. He was excited because Pink Floyd was playing that evening in town. Each year the University of Michigan had a festival on the last weekend of October and would invite known and unknown bands to play. This year it was Pink Floyd, Quicksilver and various local bands.

Morpheus had befriended one of the Floyd's roadies, Chris Adamson, who had gifted him with tickets and backstage passes to the show. He asked if we would like to go. I said, "NO, I don't think so!" Both Morpheus and Roger looked at me with disbelief and questioning surprise. Between you and me, I had grown tired of being on show. Often I rebelled by wearing ripped jeans held together at the seams with safety pins. This was just one of the things that I would do to break the image, which often did not meet with others' approval. But I continued on this way since I was a sixties child seeking not to be held down by traditional views of how I should dress or be. A new idea of freedom for women was in my heart. The sixties represented an opportunity to dare to break the mould, and in my innocence, I did, in many ways!

Ann Arbor was a town that in a similar manner sought to do just that—break the mould. It was the home of SDS—Student Demonstration Headquarters, Alice Cooper, alternative hippie stores, eccentric boutiques and a University full of young students. Our boutique, Paraphernalia, was a franchise across the US at the time and sought to lead the way through fashion. Its ethos was to encourage women to find a way of dressing that would express their individual uniqueness. On the weekends, I used to have models dressed in Carnaby fashions and Twiggy-like makeup dancing in our windows. Our boutique served as a place that would give advice to women about how to find their own identity beyond keeping up with the Joneses and being carbon copies.

In the end, Roger and Morpheus convinced me to go with them to the concert. I had just returned from NYC buyers' week so I decided to dress up. My head was still swooning from the memory of my first encounter with the world of Ossie Clark, a London fashion designer. I was touched deeply by each dress, the fabric, the colours, the femininity, the dance of the folds as the saleswoman twirled them one by one before me. I returned home enchanted and inspired even more by the London look.

That night I wore a gold and burgundy tie-dyed velvet maxi dress that I had brought back from my trip. It clung comfortably upon the young sylph-like curves of my body and the frill at the bottom would move in the wind as I walked. I also discovered Biba make-up, Twiggy-like eyelashes and lace-up leather boots. My hair was golden blonde with gentle curls to my shoulders. I was ready. We got to the concert early and found our seats in the first few rows. Morpheus and Roger left me sitting there alone while they went backstage to say hello to Chris Adamson. The last thing I wanted to do was to hang out backstage and be a groupie.

I remember looking up at the stage as the roadies scurried around working the final touches for the concert. They were so attractive with their London haircuts, tight Stirling Cooper black jeans, T-shirts, coloured boots and velvet jackets. The sound of their accents touched my heart as they shouted to one another across the stage: "Scott, can you get Peter? Can you turn up the sound?" The moment was getting closer as the roadies left the stage. The lights dimmed and the band entered. The audience went silent. The magic began with 'Embryo', 'Fat Old Sun' and David's guitar.

Rick's piano pierced the silence held by the sounds of Roger Waters' bass guitar and Nick's drums. We were spellbound as the notes carried around the audience through the Floyd's sound-in-the- round. 'Set the Controls' took us deeper, transcending us from what we knew as normal to a world where Peace and Beauty united us all that evening.

After the gig, we all went backstage. I was a rather shy person in those circumstances, and continue to be, so I often found myself standing alone in the corner while Morpheus and Roger ran around in their excitement backstage. Fortunately, one of my customers from the shop was there and we passed the time in idle chatter. Then, to my surprise, David came up to me. He had on a black T-shirt that said 'That's All Folks' and he was wearing those Stirling Cooper jeans. They all seemed to be wearing them. He was so handsome. He came close and said, "Hello, I am David." I looked up at him, his blue eyes penetrating my heart with the sound of his voice. Time stood still as I stumbled to answer.

It was as though my dream of 'love at first sight' was happening. Was he my Prince Charming? The moment held us until Morpheus and Roger broke the spell as they entered our circle. I motioned to them as I introduced myself to David: "Hello, I am Ginger and this is Morpheus, Roger and Susannah." Then I turned and left them chatting. I was so embarrassed yet stunned by David's approaching me. I sought refuge in the room where Chris Adamson was loading the equipment into the truck, hoping to regain my composure.

As I sat upon one of the road boxes chatting to Chris, Roger appeared and asked if I was open to inviting the band and the crew over the next evening for dinner. "Sure, Roger," I said, "if that's what you would like, why not?" I then went into the next room where David and the band were standing. He turned towards me, and looking him directly in the eyes, I invited HIM and the band over for roast beef and Yorkshire pudding the next evening. Roger and Morpheus were very excited that they accepted.

The following day they spent most of their time canvassing all over town for a sight of the band, hoping to confirm that they were coming. I spent most of the day preparing the meal and answering phone calls with their latest reports. As the day progressed, it became certain that our evening dinner was going to happen. The band arrived first. Roger Waters, Nick Mason and Rick Wright took their places on our long leather couch. David sat on the floor near the record player, his hair falling down over his face as he looked through our albums. He became our DJ for the evening. I was made extremely nervous by his presence, triggered by his approach the night before. Something stirred in my heart each time he came near. I was trying hard to resist an ancient calling which was summoning me.

The next day Quicksilver was playing and David and the band said they would like to go and see them. At midnight that same day, on Halloween, we were having a roller-skating party in Detroit. Roger and I invited them to come along if they wanted, schedule permitting. They accepted, so we arranged to meet them at the Quicksilver show and then go on to the party.

I was dressed in red satin hot pants and gold hearts with a full body red leotard. I was ready to go roller-skating. Roger, Morpheus and I arrived at our seats. Soon I was by myself again while they wandered backstage. Steve O'Rourke, the Floyd manager, Nick and Roger Waters arrived. Their tickets were in the row in front of me. Steve turned around, looking like Clark Kent from behind his glasses, and said to me, "Ginger, I think you should be with David." My heart nearly stopped. I managed a smile and looked away so as not to show my embarrassment.

A few minutes later, David and Peter Watts, their sound engineer, arrived. David sat right next to me with Peter following him. Someone had given them mescaline that night and David had refused to leave the hotel. He told Peter that he was so attracted to me that he didn't think he could stand being near me tripping, especially as he wasn't sure if I was in a relationship. He felt it would be difficult to resist his feelings. In the end, Peter talked him into coming.

As he sat down David placed his hand onto my leg. The lights dimmed and the music began to play. I could feel his body next to mine in the darkness. Energy surged through my being! My heart opened. I felt we were melting together just in his touch. All my life I dreamt of having a union with a man like this. I became nervous as I tried to resist the feelings that filled my body and heart. What should I do?

Roger and Morpheus reappeared before the intermission and rescued me. I asked where they had been, but before they could answer, the band said they had seen enough and wanted to go back to the hotel. We said that we would meet them there. I stood up to follow everyone. David grabbed hold of my hand, with Peter behind. At the top of the aisle, I looked at Roger and saw his glance down to where David was holding my hand. I said quietly: "He is tripping."

He said, "Don't worry. It's ok. Let's walk him back to the hotel."

So we became guardians of David. We walked hand in hand through the misty fog back to the hotel. David was holding one of my hands and Roger was holding the other. It felt strange as we each wore the mask of pretend. Ann Arbor was a miniature of Cambridge, England, where David was born and raised. It was so similar, even down to the Victorian streetlamps and the fog. He made a few comments to that regard as our journey took us through the campus.

When we got to the hotel, we met with the others, who were sitting around a table in the bar. There were two seats left. David sat down, pulling me down to sit next to him, when Morpheus arrived saying in a panic: "Rick Wright is lost." Roger P volunteered to go and find him. I stood up. He asked if I would go with him. I shook my head, saying, "Perhaps Morpheus and I should take everyone back to our house. I will meet you there." As it turned out, it was just to be Morpheus taking Roger Waters, David, and me. Everyone else would follow.

We went in Morpheus's van. It was empty in the back. Roger sat down on the floor against the back doors and so did David. I quickly sat on the wheel hub. Morpheus closed the door. It was dark. As we drove along David grabbed my hand and pulled me down into his arms. Our passion rose in our embrace. Time stood still. The van stopped with a jerk. We had reached our destination. Morpheus opened the door, and I got out first. Walking quickly towards our house, I opened the front door and darted upstairs to my bedroom. I was in tears. I was in a flurry of mixed emotions. I trembled. I felt like I was in a boat in a storm losing control. My Shih Tzu, Julie, was sitting on the bed wagging her tail. I picked her up and ran down the stairs, out of the door into the fog-lit street.

David realised that I had bolted and ran after me, catching me in his arms as I went around the corner. Our lips met. I no longer could hold back my desire to be with him—to be close to him, united in our desire. Suddenly, as though it was a bolt of lightning, a thought shouted in my head, "Oh MY GOD! What am I doing?" I pushed him away, saying in the release of our passion, "I cannot do this. I don't know you!" David said, "I do not normally do this either." So we walked back to the house, our silhouettes revealing that we were holding hands, as Roger returned, having found Rick. David could not let go.

When we got to the house, I went upstairs. Roger followed. I cried and said, "I cannot stand it! David is too attracted to me! I cannot resist. I will stay home!" I pleaded, "PLEASE. Can you take the band?" Roger said, "No, you go! I will stay." "This is impossible! We shall both go. We promised. Besides, they are waiting downstairs! I will just have to handle it." Anxiously, I ran out the door and down the stairs, as I implored him to take them. I would go in a different car! In the end, Roger did take the band in his Cadillac and I went with my assistant manager. I cried all the way. My heart was racing as we got closer to our destination.

As it was Halloween weekend, our Detroit radio station played the Orson Welles dramatisation of *War of the Worlds*. It seems that the band had never heard of it and on that evening had not listened to the introduction. By the time they reached Detroit, enhanced by the fact some were tripping, they thought the Martians had landed. What a psychic adventure that must have been, in addition to then going roller-skating. We played with reality in those days, with never a worry that not all would be well. We were explorers, daring to enter other dimensions. Casualties did happen. Syd Barrett was one.

Throughout the rest of the evening, I just skated to the music. I twirled and I jumped but I stayed my distance. Roger was looking worried and distant and if I dared stop, David would be there wanting to be close. He couldn't skate very well in his condition so Steve O'Rourke spent most of the time holding him up. Once, as I was flying past, I overheard David say to Steve, "That girl is a dream on wheels!" (Such a sweet and special memory.) All night, we went round and round the skating rink to the theme music from *Shaft*. It seemed to play over and over, along with Sly and the Family Stone's 'It's a Family Affair.' Since then, they became our theme songs from our first moments of love.

I have no idea how or when we got home. I was not sure how they made it back to their hotel either. All I remember is waking up in my bed at home. Roger and I slept in, resting from the night before, passing like ships each time we were awake. In one of those silent moments, I remember looking at the cover of *Ummagumma* on which David was sitting in the doorway. I went into a deep review of my life. The last few days had me taking a closer look at my life, as if something inside of me had awakened and things had changed.

My greatest dream was coming true. It was a dream I frequently shared with Roger. I was honest and often I had tried to leave. We were close friends. He offered a safe harbour. Looking back, I feel we were playing a part of what we thought we wanted and should do. At least I was, but I was always clear about it. He knew that I felt strongly that my Prince Charming would appear one day. Each time I shared this with him, he called me a dreamer. I was appreciative of his care, his friendship. I often thought that maybe over time I would fall in love with him in response to his kindness. However, I had a dream deep in my heart that my knight in shining armour would appear.

In the early evening, the phone rang and Roger Waters was on the other end. He wanted to speak to my Roger about playing golf the next day, as they had chatted about their mutual love of the game the previous evening. He asked if David could have a word first. I answered yes. When David got on the line, he asked if I could speak. I said, "No, not really." He suggested I just say yes or no to his questions. He asked if he could see me the next day. I said, "Yes." He then said that he would call in the morning to arrange where to meet. I then handed the phone to Roger, saying that Roger Waters wanted to ask him something about golf. In the end, it was not possible because he was leaving early on a sales trip.

David called me in the morning, knowing that I would be alone, in order to arrange where we could meet. I chose a Chinese restaurant. We spoke about the last few days. He said he still felt the same and if ever I left my relationship, which to me was in a flux, to call him. The owner of the restaurant overheard our conversation and approached us. He asked if we would like our tea leaves read. We said yes. He said, "There will be a change. There is a house with white birds across the waters." I was to come to know that David's home in England had white doves and, of course, it was across the waters.

We went back to the hotel, for it was time for David to leave. We hugged in the lobby, as everyone was there ready to go. We had a farewell kiss goodbye and he handed me a piece of paper with the phone number of his parents, who lived in NYC. His final words were, "Call me, if things change." I left and walked away feeling that I had left part of my heart behind. He waved from their car as he passed. It was a warm afternoon. The sunlight felt comforting as I walked through the town back to our boutique.

There was a sixties mystical bookshop upstairs and the manager was a close girlfriend. I shared my heart dilemma with her. She knew of all the times I had tried to leave Roger. She knew of all the times he had talked me into staying. She knew my true heart dream. Roger and I were just friends, companions. I asked her, as tears ran down my face, "Am I being dishonourable to leave without telling him face to face? I have tried so many times before. Besides, what if David and I are just a flight of fancy?"

She said, "Go! It is deeper than that."

At that moment, I realised my decision WAS deeper. I needed to follow what was deep in my heart so that I could finally live its truth. Besides, it was fair for Roger to be set free. David was just a catalyst, putting me onto the path of my soul. Going was opening the doorway to my next step. That choice was to be the first awakening to trust and act upon the divine plan awaiting in my future. Of course, I had no idea then that is what it was. God kept it a secret.

Over the next few days, I decided to leave for good and dare to go into my next adventure. I wrote out a detailed business plan of what was to come into the shop over the next six months. I paid myself my wages due to me. I called my friends Stephan and Shelley Rubin in NYC and asked if I could stay with them until I got things sorted. We were close and had spent lots of time together over the years. I told them it was over. They said, "Of course." I started packing and called the number that David had given me. His mother answered the phone. I shared with her that David had said to call if I were to come to town. I asked if she would tell him that I would be coming into the city on 5th November.

He called back. He was in Princeton, New Jersey, doing a gig, and he said he would pick me up.

Just to add to the drama, I had got a lead role in a motion picture film. It was a mixture of *Easy Rider* and *West Side Story*. My gentle and innocent nature fit the part perfectly. Because of the unseasonal rain, the directors hadn't needed me on set and no contract had been signed. Throughout the whole evening, as I did my packing, they kept calling to convince me to stay. They would give me refuge. I kept saying that I just had to go. Finally, by 4am, they said, "Alright, go, but call us when you get there." My childhood dream of being a film actress now surrendered to the meeting of my Prince Charming, which was closer to my heart.

Morpheus said he would look after Julie, my dog, until Roger returned. He would also drive me in his van to the airport. I kissed my precious Julie goodbye and left our house in Ann Arbor for good. As we went around the corner to the parallel street, which led to the freeway, Morpheus suddenly put on the brakes. I looked up through my tears, trying to focus. Two limousines were coming straight for us. One swerved and stopped in front of us, blocking the way, while the other went up onto the pavement and blocked us from behind. I panicked, trying to figure out what was going on. Flashes of James Bond went through my head as my vision cleared. Two of the directors from the movie emerged from the limos.

To my surprise, they had driven up from Detroit to make one last attempt to keep me from letting go of my role in the movie. As they approached the van, one of them said, "You can't leave!" The soft hearted one came to my window. When he saw my tears and flushed expression as I shook my head as if to say, "I can't," he said to the other, "Let her go." Looking around towards the car, he gave the driver the ok to back away and said, "Call us when you get there." We drove like the wind, and at the airport I ran, pushing four suitcases, my heart beating from the stress. I am sure passers-by could hear it. I wondered why it is that gates always seem so far away when one needs not to miss one's flight. I made it. I had no idea what my next step would be but something inside was overjoyed, relieved as I stepped on that plane.

ECHOES OF LOVE
ARRIVING IN NYC
5 NOVEMBER 1971

As I heard the steward say "Excuse me, Miss, can you fasten your seatbelt?" I started to get a bit nervous. The time had gone by so quickly. My heart was racing. Soon, we would be together… David and I.

I was one of the first to disembark and there he was, standing waiting for me to arrive. It was like a fairy tale. I pinched myself to see if it was really happening. Our eyes met and we fell into each other's arms. His hair smelled of strawberries as we came close and our hearts melted together in that moment. I couldn't stop smiling as we walked hand in hand into our future.

As it turned out, I didn't go and stay with Stephan and Shelley, only my suitcases. David and I were so in love that we could not leave each other's side, so I went on tour for his last few weeks in America. Being on the road with a rock 'n' roll band was not something I had ever thought I would do. But I felt safe in his arms.

We went straight to his hotel room. The light filtered through the voile curtains, casting a fine mist-like tone into the room. I walked over to the window and parted them to get a feeling of where we were as David sorted out the suitcases. I was entering the unknown, trusting the adventure. He came up to me from behind and held me in his arms as we looked out the window. Our souls melted, touching our destiny to be together.

Unknowingly, we surrendered to God's plan for our future, guided by his love, his protection. David had a gig that night, though I have no memory of where. All I remember is the Beauty of our first moments together. I was free to love him. Free to be loved.

We left NYC to finish his tour. They had twelve more gigs. We went to Cleveland, then Buffalo, until we reached Montreal. Every night their music was like a piece of fine silk draping over my heart tenderly. David had one of the roadies, Scott, looking after me while he was on stage. He wanted him to put a chair by their mini mixer behind the curtain on his side of the stage with a drink for me every night. Each time David was not playing guitar he would come off stage and sit me on his lap. We were constantly in each other's arms, kissing, held in a lovers' embrace.

I remember Roger's expression the first time David did this. His head hung low as he was playing his bass guitar. He looked to the right from behind his hair to find David wasn't there. He could see us in the distance hugging. Shrugging his shoulders, he continued playing. David was known to have his back to the audience when he wasn't singing, but he was always there. I think this behaviour was new for the band.

My days were magical as I entered into the world of Pink Floyd. They had hired Arthur Max to be in charge of the lights and special effects. He was so resourceful. Sometimes he went to various schools and rented equipment to enhance the beauty of the show. We got on very well. Once, during 'Echoes', which had just been released, the blue lights dimmed and I said to him, "Wouldn't it be wonderful to have snowflakes drifting gently down?" Do you know what he did? He went to a florist and got all of their old flowers, roses and chrysanthemums. During the afternoon, someone must have plucked them apart and put them into bags ready for the show. Later a roadie took them up to his post up on the rafters and let them go slowly during 'Echoes'. Such Beauty! I was happy. I kept trying to inspire him to create a rainbow, but it never happened.

MEETING THE PARENTS
NYC, CARNEGIE HALL
15 NOVEMBER 1971

I felt like a trouper by the time we came back to New York City. I had made friends with all the road crew as well. Nance Steele was a lovely girl who travelled with the crew and most nights she sat at the mixer. She was a sweetheart. I loved how David would always go out at the end of a gig and say, *"Ta Da-Night,"* waving his hands in the air. He continued to do this over the years. I loved his heart and his honour towards his team who helped make the show possible. He was gentle and caring, though most of the time he was held in his silent, quiet English way. I have experienced this aspect of English culture innumerable times; sometimes it is poetic, sometimes not, especially for an American who is used to being free with her joy and feelings. I have learned a lot being with them. I have become a universal citizen. Experiencing many other cultures and ways of being has opened my mind and heart further to love humanity, in all our unique differences. To find unity, to love and appreciate that we are all children of God with a Divine Spark waiting to shine. 'Shine On' speaks loudly to us all!

The Floyd was to play Carnegie Hall and Arthur Max had something to show them. So we had to go down near Times Square. There were workmen in a black machine that resembled a Martian space machine from the movie *War of Worlds*, which actually didn't come out until 2005.

It was a cherry picker and was used not to pick cherries but to repair streetlights and things up high on buildings or billboards. It was enormous.

Arthur arranged a demonstration for the band before they went back for rehearsals and sound check. His vision was to attach lights to them and they would move like beings, lifting from the stage, travelling over their heads. This was a YES and we grew very fond of them as they added a majestic quality to the shows. I can still hear Rick playing as they rose into the night sky. I think the Floyd were the first to use them in this context. As a result, the lorries got larger as their equipment continued to increase.

Carnegie Hall left an even deeper impression than the magic of the gig. It awakened an interest in me for architecture and the art of the twenties. I was from a Coastguard family after my mother remarried and we spent most of our time on the bases or in the shopping mall, barefoot on the weekends. I knew much more about large military boats and the Coastguard bases than this aspect of American culture, which I had never known existed. I focused more on my studies and adapting to new schools as my stepfather transferred almost every year. We drank Shirley Temples on the weekends and I danced the polka with my sister in the base cantina after catechism.

In Carnegie Hall, even the ladies' room reeked of the opulence of the twenties, with mirrors and gold everywhere. The stage had a circular part which could rise from below. Arthur made sure to use it. The music began and the Floyd seemingly appeared from below; it was an awesome moment. Out of the darkness emerged the sound of 'Set the Controls for the Heart of the Sun'. I can still hear Roger hitting the gong somewhat quietly. Rick's melodic playing, with the repetitive thumping notes of David's guitar, held us hypnotised. The lights alternated from red to blue and back again.

The tone of Roger's voice piercing the air and merging with David's "Ah-Ah-Ah" created a sound which transported us to being in an Egyptian tomb. Nick kept it all in a continuous beat, eventually building the pace. Red beacons swirled as Roger returned to the gong, madly beating it. The gong was set alight with the crashing sounds. The audience gasped, holding their breath with the tension, listening. The music drifted and fell upon us, while the only light was the flickering gong that shaped the band's silhouette. The celestial sounds took us further to the 'Heart of the Sun'. As the song quietly ended, the next one, 'Atom Heart Mother', began.

JOURNEY TO ENGLAND
NOVEMBER 5, 1971

We were somewhere between Cincinnati and Washington DC, driving to the gig. I was sitting on David's lap in the back seat when Steve O'Rourke turned around and said to me, "Well, Ginger, are you coming with us back to England?" I turned pink at the suddenness of the question and I looked at David. He said, "Do you want to?" I nodded yes as I placed my head upon his shoulders. Dreams upon dreams were coming true. Soon I would see the house across the waters with the white doves.

The moment came to live another dream… to live in England. It was really happening. We were on the plane. We held hands throughout the journey, watching a movie to pass the time. Sleeping, occasionally, in each other's arms because the flight was through the night. Morning came with the smell of coffee and bacon. I rubbed my sleepy eyes as I looked out the window at the new country I was about to know. It was like a patchwork of colour and extremely green despite the winter. Lines of colourful houses wound round the edges of the streets below with little chimney stacks and grey smoke. Swimming pools were nowhere in sight.

Warwick, a friend of David's, picked us up from Heathrow. He also cared for David's home, doing odd jobs, when he was away on tour. I found out later from Warwick that he had expected a different woman. He almost blew it by saying her name, but David had anticipated this so he quickly introduced me. The story from Warwick went like this: "The man needed a maid." Like the song from Neil Young's *Harvest*. Well, love got there first, I thought.

My English adventure had begun. The fridge was the size of an American dishwasher: rather small, and I had to stack all the leftovers and shop very cleverly to fit it all in. Fortunately, there was a cold pantry, which eventually I learned how to use. Warwick and David were little terrors some evenings after I had gone to bed. They would poke holes into the cling film that I had carefully covered the plates of food with in order to reduce the risk of food poisoning. Naughty boys! They were stoned.

From January through February, the Floyd went on tour in England. I stayed home for many gigs. Television programmes did not come on until after 4pm, by which time it was dark. We didn't have curtains or double-glazing so the winter winds would howl through the leaded light windows. I sat shivering with a blanket around me, wearing several jumpers. I was not used to being in the elements indoors. I sat each evening in David's high backed leather chair, watching whatever was on. There were only three stations, BBC 1, BBC 2 and ITV, at the time. It was snowing and a blizzard was happening outside. Brrr.

One evening, a man wearing a black coat and woollen hat peered through the living room window where I sat. He was tapping on the pane to get my attention. I absolutely freaked. Here I was alone in a foreign country with no curtains and no idea who to call… not even the police. He knocked and shouted through the howling wind, "Miss, I have brought you your water container." YIKES! The local pipes had frozen, and we were temporarily having problems with our running water. As a result, I had to bring in buckets of water from outside in the freezing cold constantly. I wondered what planet I had landed upon. Despite it all, 'What have I done?' never entered into my mind.

The adventure was still special. There were just a few bumps along the road getting used to it. I was getting a new set of tires and a new road map. I was still young, adaptable and in love, so it was easy to make it my home. This was never in any of my Sociology books. In fact, the thought of leaving the States didn't enter my mind except in my dreams. I have found that the manifestation of the dream is still different from the dream. The fridges are smaller and they drive on the opposite side of the road.

Time passed and I got used to my new home. David agreed for me to join a modelling agency and it wasn't long before I got a few modelling jobs. One year I was the face of Leichner cosmetics. I looked like a Hollywood star from the days of Marilyn Monroe and Jayne Mansfield.

It seemed I was being typecast as either a Hollywood glamour star or the innocent girl next door. Storm Thorgerson, of Hipgnosis, asked me to be on the cover of one of Al Stewart's albums, *Modern Times*. I knew Storm well since he did the Floyd's album covers and was an early Cambridge friend of David's. The photo shoot was in the garden of an English manor house early in the morning. Al Stewart was sitting in a Cord automobile owned by Jimmy Page from Led Zeppelin. I was wearing a sequinned maxi slinky dress in the likeness of a twenties Hollywood star with a lynx fur coat. I was running away from him after the night before, pretending it was warm; but it was not. Early morning shoots were always my least favourite. The lighting was great, but it was cold!

Chateau d'Hérouville

OBSCURED BY CLOUDS
CHATEAU D'HÉROUVILLE
FRANCE 1972

The Floyd accepted a request to write the music for a soundtrack for a French film, *La Vallee,* by Barbet Schroeder. It was the first time that I had ever visited a foreign speaking country. The album was recorded at Strawberry Studios at Chateau d'Hérouville, just outside Paris. All of the crew stayed with us at the Chateau including Puddy, Pete Watts' girlfriend. The schedule for the Floyd was very intense, watching the film repeatedly. They did not have time to make long dreamy songs like 'Echoes.' In the end, the album was created in just two weeks.

We ate, slept and recorded there in the Chateau. Puddy and I spent a lot of time riding the Metro to French markets. After one outing, when we returned to the Chateau wearing our new fluffy, imitation fur platform boots, Nick Mason commented, "You girls should get in a bit of culture."

It was the first time that I had ever heard that word. "Culture... what is that, Nick?" we both asked, getting a bit flushed with embarrassment because of the innuendo in the tone of his voice. "You know, a few museums and galleries and monuments. Perfect place for it," he said. Admittedly and perhaps indignantly, we didn't do it that time. Since then, I have become a serious culture buff. I have become a messenger for the need of culture and Beauty and its importance for maintaining world peace.

DARK SIDE OF THE MOON
GOES ON THE ROAD
JAPAN TOUR 1972

Between the two weeks it took to record the album, the Floyd did gigs in Japan. It was a long, long flight. Most of us took some mandies (mandrake), a form of happy sleeping pill, which always made me giggle until I fell asleep. Japan was different from France. Some might call it a culture shock for this American at the time, and perhaps it was for them as well; however, this was their second trip. I often felt we were living a modern-day *Shogun*, walking down the streets with our long hair and different accents.

When we first arrived at the airport, there was a banner hanging over the door at the terminal saying, 'Welcome PINK FROYD'. The Japanese had difficulty in pronouncing our L and it seems even writing it. We had to take a large bus to our hotel and David was sitting next to the window. There was a surge of people towards the bus, flashing cameras everywhere.

David noticed that one of the girls had forgotten to take off her lens cap so he was pointing to her through the window that separated them, trying to tell her. She got so excited that he had acknowledged her that she did not notice until the bus drove away. She slumped in a pile of tears at the lost opportunity. No photos but she did have a memory that David Gilmour had acknowledged her.

The tour started in Tokyo, a bustling city mixed with many cultures and large billboards with flashing lights. Finding McDonald's in Tokyo amazed me. I gave it a try and everything tasted like fish. Not at all the taste I was accustomed to. One evening our promoter took us out for a special Japanese dinner. Women in beautiful kimonos served us as we sat on the floor. Thank God we had to remove our knee-high platform boots before sitting down because I fear that it would have been impossible to sit in them, as I was also wearing very tight jeans. They were so tight in those days that I had to lie down on the bed to zip them up.

The evening began as we sat on the floor atop fine pillows made from Japanese silk. Warm saké, green and brown teas alternating between each course to cleanse our palates. I had never eaten raw fish before, never mind octopus tentacles. Over the years, I have come to love raw fish, but not the octopus tentacles. Through this experience a seed was planted that would become my future way of eating—simple, beautiful and sacred. Our trip also inspired an interest in the art of bonsai, which further led me to appreciate and admire the Japanese philosophy in the Art of Living.

On this tour, the Floyd were testing out *Dark Side of the Moon* in preparation to record it when they got home. On the first night, the audience did nothing after each song. We didn't understand because the gig was super. One thing we had to adjust to was that Japanese audiences showed no emotion during the concert. Puddy and I were a bit perplexed for we were used to the American audiences, who freely expressed their feelings. Stadiums were lit by the little flames of their lighters; I always loved it. Thousands of them adding to the beauty they had just heard.

Once the gig was finished, though, and the last note played, the audience went berserk! Their behaviour was like chalk and cheese. Wild frantic clapping accompanied with screams and tears of rapture filled the air. Like ants that fled their broken nest, they descended towards the mixer. The roadies and sound engineer, Peter Watts, surrounded us and got us to safety backstage. Phew; but it was not over.

As we left the back of the hall where our limos were waiting, they descended, trying to get to their stars in a mad fervour. I pushed David into the car before me, blocking their grasping hands trying to grab his T-shirt. I became his protector. My lioness arose from the depth of my heart to enable me to have the strength to stop them until he reached the safety of the limo. The drivers had the engines ready to go once we were all safely inside. The limos slowly pierced the desperate waiting crowd in convoy. Their hands were wiping against the windows as we left them behind, making our way back to the hotel. I began to understand a bit about what

The Beatles had experienced every day from the mania stirred from their idolatry as my adrenaline calmed.

The next gig was in Kyoto. The Floyd made a mad dash to the reception because they had discovered that there were some traditional Japanese rooms in each hotel. They were like little boys. Every time we checked into a new hotel, it became a game. David got one for us this time. It was a special experience. The hotel had been a traditional shogun mansion which was converted. As we entered our room, silent tranquillity started to touch my soul with its Beauty. There was a traditional garden with glass sliding doors and a miniature water feature. A sunken, square bath you had to sit in instead of lying down. We slept on a futon on the bamboo matted floor which rolled up in the morning after we went out for the day.

We travelled on to Sapporo for the next gig. Sapporo hosted the 1972 Winter Olympics. Therefore, the band decided that they would love to have a go at skiing down the slope. David wasn't much of a skier then, but was obviously fearless, or perhaps stupid, since he decided to have a go. I stayed at the bottom and watched him inch his way as he traversed the Olympic slope while keeping his fingers crossed. Their long hair was blowing in the wind and snow, resembling The Beatles from afar. Luckily, they all made it down without injury. I do not believe their insurance company would have favoured the lark, but it was a good boyish laugh.

When we got back to the UK, they still had to finish *Obscured by Clouds* but continued working on *Dark Side of the Moon*. Once the final recording was on vinyl, they took it on tour again. They preferred to review new material on stage, developing it to their satisfaction, gauging their performance as well as the audience's reaction, before committing to recording the new music. Unfortunately, there appeared lots of bootleg albums, which eventually changed this practice.

SUMMER IN LINDOS
RHODES, GREECE
1973

Every morning I awake with such inspiration to continue writing my memoirs. My heart is opening as the moments of Beauty and Love return to me. On this morning I was pondering the time we, most of the band, all went to Lindos, Rhodes, Greece. David rented a pea green E-type and we set off from London driving across Europe. We stopped to visit his parents first, who were having their summer holiday in Ramatuelle, a French village just outside St. Tropez. I still remember the sounds of the swallows as they flew in between the stone buildings above me. "They never land on the ground," David told me.

We travelled towards our destination through the mountains of Switzerland. The car was a convertible and with the wind in our hair, we laughed in the sunshine as we drove along. I loved looking at David, his hair, his eyes. Was this really happening? It was as though we had been in love before, through lifetimes of togetherness. The landscape was so majestic it took my breath away. We stopped for little bites of cheese and bread and a glass of wine along the way. I had never had such wonderful wine in my life as I did on this journey.

We drove on to Brindisi, Italy, where we took a boat to Patras, Greece. I felt a little seasick in our room below from the fumes and the loud churning sound of the engine. Consequently, I had to spend most of the journey up on deck. We left the car in Patras and flew to Rhodes. We arrived in the early evening. The sun was setting as we walked down the stairs of the aeroplane. The air was full of the scent of orange blossom mixed with sage, rosemary and thyme travelling on the warmth of the Mediterranean breeze as it tousled our hair.

I stopped for a moment upon the stairs to allow it to enter and refresh my soul. That night was to be the first journey of many that we were to take down the island of Rhodes to Lindos, for we eventually bought a house, actually two. One is in Lindos and the other was further down the island in Pefkos, Lindos, which became home away from home for many years. It was a place where we could relax and safely raise our children on holiday. We taught them how to swim and be free. Now, after nearly forty years, we have become part of the community, growing old together.

That evening we took a taxi from the airport. As you round the last corner just before you get to Lindos from Rhodes, the view still takes my breath away, especially at night. The village twinkles with the streetlights through the orange trees and the boats in the bay light up the harbour like Christmas. In the distance, you can hear the cicadas and the rustling of the leaves. Night flowering jasmine, orange and lemon trees create a floating fragrance. The stillness takes one into another reality of time. Storybooks are written upon such magical beauty, set off by the stars in the sky. The Knights' Castle's silhouette is revealed each night by the light of the rising orange moon. And there we were, in love, holding hands, held captive in a timeless moment.

Our first summer, we stayed with the Floyd manager and his family: Steve and Linda O'Rourke and their two children, Kate and Shanna. They had rented one of my favourite Knights' houses, owned and restored by Sandro and Patrizia Somare. Sandro was an Italian painter from Milan, who worked closely with an Italian architect. Together they restored it from being a derelict donkey stable to its former glory as a Knight's residence with an Italian flavour. Many of the older houses built centuries ago were for the Knights.

Sandro's house had a traditional two storey stone wall, which surrounded the property and gardens. We entered in through a huge wooden door in the middle to find a wooden dinner table in the courtyard all aglow with candles and a feast. Everyone was there that had arrived in town from England. Juliette and Rick Wright had rented a separate house in the village that year. They had no idea that Steve had rented one at the same time. I think they had expected and hoped to have time away from the other members of the band.

Some of their other friends had joined us during our holiday: Germaine Greer, David Hockney, Tony Howard and his wife, Nancy, but they stayed with Melissa North-Tchassey in number 24 down the road from us. Melissa had worked with Tony Howard and Steve for many years and is probably the person who inspired them to come there. Another friend, Tony Gorvitch, stayed with us for some of the time in Sandro's villa. He was another rock 'n' roll manager.

I entered, that summer, an entirely different world from middle America. I was so green and innocent; but ready to discover my destiny full of joy. I was impressionable and easily inspired by those who were creating Beauty. And the world I had entered stimulated my own innate creativity. I was so in love that being in the unknown was OK. There was so much to learn and to experience. Life was taking me on a fast track onto my future path of being an artist creating Beauty, unbeknownst to me. I listened. I observed. I went with the adventure. I smiled, I laughed, I cried. I trusted my life.

THE ROSE CITY, MARRAKECH
GINI PHOTO SHOOT 1972
FRENCH TOUR 1974

A French soft drink company who produced a bitter lemon drink called Gini approached the Floyd to do some advertising for them. It was to be the first of its kind for the Floyd to allow the use of their image in a publicity campaign. It would prove to be an embarrassment later, but it seemed at the time to be a lucrative adventure. But hey, we would get to go to Morocco and be in the magical Rose City of Marrakech. David and a few friends had gone before and spoke of it highly. The only bad memory was the food poisoning from something they had eaten.

Gini booked us into the famous La Mamounia Hotel, which previously had been a historical palace of the Rose City, and was converted into a luxurious hotel. As we entered the lobby of mosaics and carved plasterwork, a man was walking away down one of the corridors. He had long hair and was wearing a Hawaiian shirt. I commented to David that he looked a bit like Mick Jagger. David said whimsically, "That may be because it is Mick Jagger!" Being in the presence of all these rock legends was very new to me. I only ever saw them on telly, in a magazine or at a concert. And everything any of us, the normal public, knew about them was from the music papers and gossip. Here I was within their world.

We had the afternoon to explore amongst all the alleyways and bazaars. Everywhere was lined with tradesmen who tried to lure us to buy their carpets or wares. It was a bustle of tourists and a mixture of many cultures, Arabian, African and European. One could only enter its mystery by walking deeper and deeper amongst the pink-terracotta walls and the scent of spices. Each corner spoke of its history reminiscent of a bygone era nestled at the base of the Atlas Mountains. Didn't I tell you I had become a culture buff?

By the time we had returned to the hotel there was word that Mick Jagger wanted to be our tour guide and would take us to a very exotic but hidden restaurant in the centre of Marrakech. It was his favourite and not many would find it without help. He had a car and a driver. We all took taxis. There was a copper triple-tiered water fountain at the entrance. The sound of water seems to be part of the culture of Morocco, perhaps a symbol representing its precious value and importance to life while in the desert. Every drop as it cascades down to the bottom pool refreshes to then return and start again. The circle of life in its presence sings its song.

After dinner, Mick suggested that we should go to one of his favourite discotheques. He said that David and I should come with him in his car and arranged another taxi for the rest of our party. He suggested that they should follow. Well, his driver drove like he was in Milan and the other car could not keep up. Their taxi disappeared as we drove through the ancient streets. I often wondered if that was intentional and Mick just wanted us.

Once we entered the club, Jagger danced most of the evening in the centre of the crowd, pawed repeatedly. We watched from our table in the corner. He, with raised arms, swirled with the music. The rhythmic beat carried all to a fervour upon their heightened adulation. It was like a scene out of *Suddenly, Last Summer* where Katherine Hepburn's son was walking up the white streets into the sun with all these men admirers pawing him lustfully to his demise. The local fans devoured Mick and he loved it! When we returned to the hotel, some of the band were in the lobby. They wondered what had happened to us. David just shrugged his shoulders and did a David sheepish smile as we walked away holding hands, returning to our room.

The next morning, we had to drive out of the city and into the desert. For miles and miles, the vast colours of earth surrounded us. It was hot and dusty as we drove along the dirt roads further away from civilisation. At one point we came upon a billboard in the middle of the nowhere saying Timbuktu 52 miles by camel. It was a T-junction in the sand. Our driver turned left. We were in convoy followed by the film crew. Finally, we reached our next hotel where we were to stay until the photo shoot was finished. I think it was for two or three days.

We had breakfast and resumed our journey further into the desert. What was amazing to me was that even though we seemed alone in this vast desolate space in the middle of nowhere three African boys came walking up. They were curious as to what was going on. I suppose they saw our dust trails and followed them.

One of the evenings, the promoters arranged a special dinner and a traditional Moroccan concert. We sat outside on pillows covered in traditional tapestries before low wooden tables. A feast awaited us. Terracotta plate after plate kept coming, full of traditional delicacies. I was so worried that we might have to eat raw eyeballs from some local animal. I felt this way because earlier Steve had told me that it was a delicacy and if we turned it down, our host would take it as an insult. I am not sure whether Steve was winding me up, but fortunately, this did not happen.

The evening started to cool and a fresh, gentle breeze came over from the desert. The night was silent and we could see the stars above. From behind the building entered a long line of very tall men dressed in white robes. They were majestic as the Masai, with skin colour deep and rich like the earth. As the music played, they sang in high voices the songs of the desert. At the same time, their clapping alternated in a repetitive melodic rhythm as each bent over one by one, undulating like a wave upon the ocean. It was beautiful and hypnotic.

The French tour was in 1974 and the photographic session was in 1972. Two years after the Gini shoot, the Floyd did five gigs in France, which turned out to be diabolical. They had forgotten that their contract with the French company entitled them to advertise and sell the drink at each gig. The idea of what the promotion would be from the ad agency was beyond what fit within the image of the Floyd. Needless to say, it did not sit easily with their fans either. They coveted the image of the Floyd as being an underground group. Consequently, Steve O'Rourke, their manager, worked at bridging the growing gap between the band and Gini. The oversight did not go over well with the Floyd. So many times, I felt sorry for him being the punching bag, the go-between. But that was to be only the beginning.

At each gig, a circus of trendy, groovy people sporting leather jackets and dark glasses carrying Gini bitter lemon signs bombarded the show.

There were painted vans, banners and *Easy Rider* bikers. The road crews were thrilled because there was a collection of page three models baring their breasts who kept them company in the evenings. Steve O'Rourke was constantly negotiating how to keep them away or at least at a safe distance. Besides a distraught Floyd, the fans were also very bothered by the whole bravado. This was not their Pink Floyd.

So we went from gig to gig with our Gini entourage, the Floyd embarrassed and feeling guilty for they thought they had taken easy money. They decided to give what they had earned away to charity. Was this easy absolution? No idea. For the fans, some of the glitter wore off around their idols, which I don't think was so bad.

It was a reality check for them all, including the Floyd. I know the band looked at it deeply. Were they creating or being inspired by music that transcends, or was it the glamour of being a star or an audience taken by idol worship? Who knows? Good stuff really. The affair served to challenge everyone to question what it was all about.

KATE BUSH
MAN WITH THE CHILD IN HIS EYES
1973-1975

Between touring and working with Roland Petite, David had converted one of the outbuildings into his studio. This enabled him to do more work, as he was no longer inside the house with less equipment. The band was having some time off and both Nick Mason and David were open to taking on various projects while. Roger worked on the beginning of *Pros and Cons of Hitch Hiking* and what later became *The Wall*. Initially, David used this time to record his first solo album, which he was to call *David Gilmour*. Rick Wills and Willie Wilson, who were old friends and played with David in his Cambridge band, The Jokers Wild, joined in the creative adventure.

The snowdrops were just beginning to show their faces when Storm Thorgeson came to take photos for the album cover. He focused on having us stand in various positions in the garden. Eventually, they all went over to France to finish recording and producing at Superbear Studios. Some of the songs still play in my head: 'No Way Out Of Here', 'When You Are In You Are In For Good'. I often wonder if some of the lyrics were a foreboding of things to come. Carl Jung said that artists often express their feelings or subconscious thoughts through their music. That was how David spoke of things not said.

One day David met up with Rick Hopper and brought home a cassette of songs from a young singer-songwriter, Kate Bush. She was just fifteen and still in school. Her music inspired him to do a demo, initially recorded at Woodley in his new studio. He was helping Unicorn to get kickstarted and enlisted two of the musicians to help. David had such heart and a drive to not only develop his career, but also to use his talent for others.

Kate would arrive, still in her school uniform, and they would record her songs. She and I grew to be great friends. Woodley had a little fish pond in the front garden with a large willow tree where often we would sit and chat. I felt like her big sister. As time passed, the little schoolgirl grew into a woman. Some still say that the 'The Man With The Child In His Eyes' carried love for David. He helped her so greatly. I was not surprised that her admiration and gratefulness would hold an element of love. He seemed to take her under his wing as an uncle would do, ensuring her safety. We all did.

Just before we were to marry, as I reflect upon our life events, David helped Kate further. While the Floyd were recording *Wish You Were Here* in 1975, he presented a more finished demo of Kate's to Bob Mercer, managing director of EMI, who then signed her to EMI Records. Her passion and talent was born and time passed as we watched it create a star.

It was to be many years later that Kate and I were to meet again, but under different circumstances. In the early 90s I was working with Lily Cornford in a healing clinic. Lily was like everyone's ideal fairy godmother with a heart of gold. After one of our sessions, I walked into the waiting room and there was Kate. It was like our lives had come full circle. I had no idea that they were good friends, though fairy godmothers do get around. Kate wrote a song for her which is featured on her album *Red Shoes*. Each day we could hear it drifting from Lily's private room upstairs as she had her cup of tea and cucumber sandwiches. A haunting voice of tragedy and love.

GONNA GET MARRIED
7 JULY 1975

During the second leg of the American tour in 1975, I stayed behind. David asked if I would drive him to the airport. I said that I would, but that it most probably would be the last time. Getting to Heathrow from Essex around the North Circular can be painful when your heart is aching. I really missed him when he went off without me. We hugged goodbye and I went home. A week later, I decided to go to Lindos with two girlfriends, Cyndy Shirley, wife of Jerry Shirley, drummer of Humble Pie, and her girlfriend, Sharon, who had just come over from the States. We would stay in Melissa's house with another one of their friends, Tony, a roadie for Humble Pie, who would join us.

I was sick with bronchitis most of the time and observed the girls from my window in the sala in their tight silk Chinese dresses and high heels dancing in the courtyard. Ghetto-blaster blaring, a bit drunk with a few Greek soldiers, they were. The courtyards in Lindos are made of pebbles upright called Kuklaki. I could not figure out how they could dance without catching their heels between the stones. Maybe they floated? Anyway, they did; that is, they danced in high heels without injury.

During my time getting better, I drifted in and out of thoughts and feelings about maybe leaving David. So when I got home this was very much on my mind. What had started out as a dream come true was now changing. It seemed that a broken heart loomed in the corner. David called from the States and asked if I would pick him up the next day. I reminded him of my last statement about doing that. He said, "*Please*." So I did. I waited at the arrival point for him to come out full of alternating emotions. I was excited but nervous. Happy yet hurt. Most of the band were first. They smiled as they passed by, anxious to get home, disappearing into the crowd.

When David appeared, he walked straight up to me, gently pushing me up against the nearby wall in a passionate embrace. With the return of his passion, I was stunned. Apparently, rumour has it he had had a fair amount to drink on the plane and had flirted with one of the royals. But here it was, an embrace so big that it opened my heart once again. He was good at sending love just whenever I was having a turn away. His timing was always perfect. And it worked for many years. It certainly worked that day.

Warwick McCredie had become their personal road manager for the tours. As he was a dear friend and neighbour, we gave him a lift home. He drove and stopped for petrol on the North Circular. When Warwick went in to pay, David asked me to marry him. I could not believe my ears. The day was warm and sunny, so we lay in the garden sharing stories. We were so happy to be together, close, at home, when again he asked me to marry him. I hadn't responded earlier with Warwick returning to the car. Truly, I was a bit in shock. I couldn't believe it. Did David actually propose? I questioned myself years later as to why I said yes, for my heart had been so let down. But there I was, nestled in his arms, and I said, "Yes." I really wanted the dream to be real and continue, and it did. Another cycle began for us.

The Floyd had a gig at Knebworth on July 5th. It was a sunny afternoon. We all sat on blankets on the grass backstage, listening to the music as each band played. Stevie Miller, Captain Beefheart, Roy Harper, Linda Lewis, Monty Python. The Floyd were to play in the evening. They had just flown back from the second half of their *Dark Side of the Moon* tour in the States so there was a bit to organise for the jet-lagged roadies.

Backstage was very civilised, with marquees and caravans. The English weather did accommodate and helped the ambience of the day. As the music held us in the palm of its hand, the umbrellas stayed closed. Some brought picnics, others ate at the concession stands. The sunshine was bliss and its warmth relaxed our bodies; we were grateful there was no traditional English rain. We lay on blankets on the lawn enjoying the moment together.

Finally, the time arrived when the circular screen was up and the sound system was ready. They hoped. It took ages to set all the gear up. It wasn't as straightforward because the equipment was wounded, on top of which all the other acts were using the Floyd sound system as well. The roadies had to start early despite their jet-lag. I must admit, the audience deserved a merit badge for patience, waiting for the day of music to begin. Thank God the weather was wonderful.

It seems that on the last North American gig an overzealous crew member decided that the easiest way to dispose of the remaining explosives was to attach them to the stadium's illuminated scoreboard. And then fire them off. The explosion was devastating. The board exploded into smoke and flames while the air was filled with thousands of floating scoreboard numbers. Not only did the Floyd have to pay for a replacement scoreboard but it had shattered many neighbourhood windows!

For Knebworth, the road crew were still struggling when the scheduled fly pass of two Second World War spitfires buzzed the unsuspecting audience and the band. They were a bit unprepared and rushed in to starting. Timing was out but it still served to stun the audience into quiet attention as it always did. Unfortunately, the performance was not up to their normal standard. It dragged, probably because of their jet-lag and equipment failure, and Roger sang out of tune. The fans were sad. The press were relentless. Rick's Hammond failed and he walked off stage.

The UK press knocked them again as they always seemed to do over the years. They complained that they let down their country for appearing infrequently. They were getting boring as they played the same songs again. However, despite the press, the American tour sold out, to the surprise of many, and so did this one. It was a mystery to them that this underground group was selling out faster than The Stones.

At Knebworth, a sea of heads again sat before us, many more than were allowed for by the promoter's licence. The perimeter fences came down to care for the large numbers: over 100,000 turned out instead of the 40,000 expected. Their profile had expanded since 'Money', forcing them to do larger venues. On top of this, they and the management needed the money. Large concerts were more lucrative and they had the Norton Warburg affair looming to resolve.

There was a growing feeling of agitation after the American tour. The growing numbers and the noise from their American fans' jubilation was changing the intimacy of what went before. It was becoming more a rave party and not a concert whose intention was to take you on a journey. No longer could the subtleties of 'Echoes' be heard. The cheering drowned the spaces between the notes. The alienation and the questioning of why they were doing this began to enter their conscious minds, especially Roger's. The screaming could be deafening. The frustration of the waste of it all was loud in our hearts. Where had the Beauty gone? No longer to be heard.

Roger is quoted as saying, "I cast myself back into how f***ing dreadful I felt on the last American tour with all those thousands and thousands and thousands of drunken kids smashing each other to pieces. I felt dreadful because it had nothing to do with us. I didn't think there was any contact between us and them" (*Pink Floyd Lyric Book*, Blandford, 1982). In a peculiar way, this experience would later inspire the albums *Animals* and *The Wall*. However, for now, the return to an English audience was refreshing, except that the gig did not turn out quite as they had wanted.

The USA tour and Knebworth were behind us. Our life began to melt together in a more established home life mixed with the Floyd's growing fame as time passed. When I had said yes to coming to live with David, I had no idea that "Yes" really had to do with something else. It had to do with saying "Yes" to something growing inside of me that would take many years to awaken, i.e. my own innate calling to be an artist.

I was instinctively inspired by the creative power of the band, especially David's guitar playing and his voice. Living with a musician and loving a musician was such an adventure. Creativity surrounded me on many levels, which encouraged my own artistic development. I was a witness to David's music as it was being given birth to, plus his support for other musicians. Music was all around me some days twenty-four seven. It wasn't just listening to a record or the radio. It was in the air I breathed. My dreams were escalating from the dreams of a young girl to the life of a woman. No longer was I simply existing, yearning for love and creativity. It was my life. I started to create sculptures. They were tiny at first. Little pink resin roses for Christmas presents. Watercolours and clay forms fired in Judy Waters' kiln in London.

Most of all our love triggered an internal desire to create a child. So many times, I whispered softly in his ear that when he was ready I was ready to make a baby. I could not have dreamt of doing anything else but that at the time. My body screamed to have our child. But it seemed that we were drifting apart. A fear crept into my being. The fire was dimming a bit. It worried me. Living with a musician in a band was new to me. One day he was there, the next he was on tour or recording.

I was not always aware of the tensions growing in the band. Moreover, I was not aware just how much of that tension subtly influenced our relationship. David kept most of these matters to himself. It is only now, reading some of the stories, that I realise more of what went on behind the scenes of our life. But the instinctive impulse to bear a child from our love remained the same, as something seemed to grow quiet between us. Or was it just the process of time, merging the hearts of two individuals and the blending of two cultures? And a rock 'n' roll band? I loved him, that was for sure. Does one ever know about the cycles of love for the first time? We were young, learning about life.

The Floyd were recording *Wish You were Here* at Abbey Road Studios in the afternoon, so David arranged the paperwork needed to get married in the UK in the morning. The Floyd had the gig at Knebworth on the 5th July, so our wedding plans were for the 7th July 1975. Afterwards David had to go to Abbey Road to continue recording *Wish You Were Here.* I went with him so that we could share the day together. The band had no idea until we walked in. There always seem to be stories within stories in our life. You will see why as you read further. Just to add to the day's events, when we arrived, Roger walked up to David, pulling him aside, and whispered to him, "Look who is sitting on the sofa." They both went slowly over to the place Roger was referring to, Nick and Rick following discreetly.

There was a huge sofa in front of the mixing desk in that EMI recording room. I don't think any of them were completely certain who was sitting there until David confirmed it. David looked and his face clouded over with the reality of what he saw. Under his breath, he said, "It's Syd." The atmosphere in the room went silent as they digested the moment. Roger, especially, who is quoted to have had many mixed emotions about the past flooding back, was quiet.

There was Syd, pear shaped, hairless and overweight. They stood silently in disbelief. Old memories rushed into their hearts. What had happened? His timing was uncanny! Their lost love and the tragedy of Syd had inspired the creation of 'Shine On'. And there they were in the middle of recording it when Syd appeared, weather worn and without hair. They stumbled to have a conversation, inviting him to listen to a track. Syd just sat there, lost, on the sofa, wondering why. What a day to ponder. What a day to remember. Silence filled the room where just before music had played.

Memories floated across the night in whispers behind the studio walls. I wanted to know more about this man who sat there. The stories all began around the beginning and explained why David was now in the band and Syd was gone. A dear childhood friend of David's from Cambridge, Emo, was living with us at the time, and he told me the story. He was there when it all happened and he was a great storyteller. So over the next few days the pieces of the puzzle began to fit.

David had gone to France in 1966–68 with Willie Wilson and Rick Wills. They were gigging together, not as Jokers Wild, but as The Flowers. Emo moved to London to Calvedon Rd in 1967. Pip stayed in Cambridge. David returned to London in 1968 and moved in with Emo. They both got jobs working for Ossie Clark at Quorum in Chelsea. David drove the van and Emo put the studs on the leather jackets. They met so many colourful people. London was alive.

Emo was close to Syd during his time in London. Their friendship carried over from Cambridge. LSD was the drug of choice, but it was pure. Emo said that after the Floyd American tour in 1968, Syd returned in a very bad way. It is said that he had gone to a party in the States and was given some really bad acid. The trip was one of Syd's worst nightmares, from which he would never recover. His deepest fears came out and as a result he became really mentally strung out and ill.

Syd was interested in the teachings of R.D. Laing, a Scottish psychiatrist, who wrote extensively on mental illness. His main premise which influenced Syd was "break on through to the other side." Syd did try. Storm, Dave, Gale, Nigel, and Ponji arranged for Syd to have one on one sessions with R.D. Laing. He only had two sessions because it was too challenging. He continued taking LSD. Instead of breaking through to the other side, he went into a black hole.

One could still have conversations with him at times. Other times it was impossible. He was gone. He often wandered through the streets of

Chelsea and Kensington, where everyone lived and hung out. It got worse and worse. He couldn't play anymore. He would often just stand on the edge of the stage and stare at the audience. The band tried to hold him together and kept bringing him to gigs. Eventually, Emo said, it got too painful for him to watch. He stopped going to the gigs.

David and Emo were living in a new flat in Warwick Square Mews when Roger Waters called to speak with David. They knew each other from Cambridge. Emo was sitting on the bed when David came into the room after the call and said, "The Floyd have asked me to play in the band!" "Wow! Then you don't have to drive a van anymore!" Emo exclaimed, rather excitedly. They jumped around the room together like two maniacs. When they both came back to sanity, David casually said, "But Roger said I had to dress like a pop star. What should I do?" Emo responded, "Well, dress like a pop star!" "Well, how do I do that?" David wondered. Emo suggested: "We can go to Ossie Clark. He has the clothes that pop stars wear." David rolled his eyes, realising that he had been delivering the clothes all the time.

Ossie dressed David in a black ruffled shirt and brown skintight velvet trousers. David had maroon Gohill boots already, which really went with the outfit. He did look rather camp and played it up a bit in the shop after hours. It was not quite his style—David was slightly embarrassed for he was more at home in blue jeans—but he transcended it. Getting the job was a gift he had desired. The rest is history.

Emo remembers the day that David returned from America, in 1971, and brought me with him to the flat in Warwick Way. I was so shy and innocent. He said David was really proud and showed me off. I had no idea. He said it was evident how much we were in love. We were always kissing and holding hands. To Emo, the beauty of David's face could launch a thousand ships and he found the same in mine. He could tell we were a match made in heaven.

Personally, I remember feeling at that time like I had walked into the movie *Blow Up*. It was a movie depicting the swinging life in London, inspired by the real life of London photographer David Bailey. My life was to become just that and I loved it. Well, part of it. I really missed home. Fortunately, many new friendships were born and lasted a lifetime of challenges, laughter and tears.

PARADISE ON YOUNG ISLAND
CARIBBEAN
1976

The band was building and designing Britannia Row, which would be their own private studio where they could work in seclusion. Therefore, David and I decided to go away to St. Vincent in the West Indies. I was six months pregnant and still ok to fly. We were to stay on a private island near St. Vincent called Young Island. All the rooms were little self-contained huts. Our showers were outdoors in a private garden similar to at Lindos in Greece. We ate in the open air restaurant amongst the sweet songbirds and the fragrance of the flowers.

I had my first papaya with fresh lime juice and a pineapple coconut smoothie each morning for breakfast. The westward winds kept us cool as we baked in the sun. Steel bands played in the night from across the waterway, which separated us from the main island. We could hear voices singing their country anthem, 'St. Vincent, Land so Beautiful', drifting across the gentle winds, along with the melodies of reggae.

Often we would go across to the mainland in a little covered motorboat provided for people who stayed at Young Island. We took a local taxi and went on adventures into their forests to various gardens and sites. The island of St. Vincent is volcanic and includes little level ground. The windward side of the island is very rocky and steep, while the leeward side has more sandy beaches. In 1902–1903, devastating volcanic eruptions from La Soufrière on St. Vincent hindered the agricultural abundance, and over time, the volcanic lava formed black sand. Our first trip was to the black sand beach.

After a long drive, we came around a corner where before us lay the volcanic black sand beach sparkling in the sunlight. We walked barefoot among its crystalline form. I played with it between my toes and fingers, watching the sunlight twinkle in my hands. It was hotter than normal sand. The black colour absorbed the heat so we could not stay barefoot for long. Its unique beauty remains in my memories like black crystal.

As we both loved to snorkel and be one with the water, we decided to purchase the necessary gear to do so. Just beneath the twinkling satin surface of the Caribbean water is a world of wonder. Schools of fish of a thousand different shapes and colours lie below its surface. One would never know unless you entered. The rays of sunlight that filtered into this underground world played upon all the colours as we swam amongst the fish and the coral. Little pufferfish with their puckered-lips would come up to us, hovering, seemingly wondering who we were. They are gentle beings who, when frightened, blow up to double their size. We swam so as not to disturb them. Angelfish and seahorses carried by the current would pass by amongst the splendour.

We were lost in this wonderland for hours when it was time for us to return. We had stayed around the water between Young Island and the mainland thinking it was safe. We didn't notice that the current was getting stronger as the afternoon tide was changing. We were strong swimmers with our flippers but on this occasion, I wasn't. I was pregnant and the flow was too strong for me to make it back. I was losing strength and about to pass out when the fear gripped me, imagining myself swept out to sea. Terrified, I shouted to David for help. I do not know to this day where he got his strength. He held on to me and we swam and swam against the tide as the waves splashed in our faces. We were exhausted by the time we returned but alive. Our baby was safe!

Our time at Young Island was ending and it was time to fly home as the Floyd was about to start recording again. Britannia Row should be ready, leaving behind the times of recording at Abbey Rd. The blue skies and colours of the islands faded into the horizon as our plane flew into the clouds above. I loved being pregnant and flying seemed easy. I slept as David watched some of the movies during our journey home, turning from time to time, holding his hand.

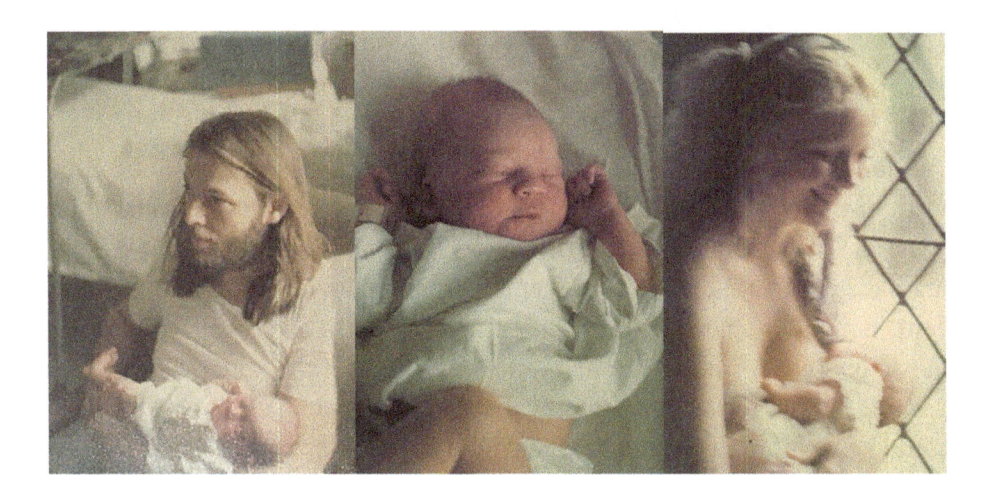

BABY ALICE IS BORN
LONDON
8 MAY 1976

In the beginning, before our trip to Young Island, it came to pass one summer that one of my deepest wishes was to come true. Earlier I shared moments with you of me held in David's arms, moments when I whispered to him, "David, when you are ready I would love to have your children." I had such a calling for our love to bring a wonderful soul into being. My body ached with the desire. We were in Lindos for the summer, staying in one of the Knights' houses of old. We returned there for many summers as its majestic beauty went deeper into our being.

This summer was our second return to Lindos and became part of many Greek adventures. Melissa was giving a party that evening and we all had to wear white. During the daytime, we went out on Carla's boat until the sunset. The water was crystal with golden reflections of the setting sun. I loved those moments. I would always sit at the front of the boat feeling the brightness of the gold upon my face.

Ossie Clark was staying with Melissa and was giving everyone LSD. We decided to join in. I remember sitting on the wall overlooking the bay. The moon sparkled on the water creating new patterns with the ripples. Melissa had placed many mattresses for us to lie on in the courtyard. There was a grapevine across part of it that dripped light green shapes onto me as I gazed into the starlit sky above. Being a person with an artistic imagination, I always had acid trips that were visual. They were always full of Beauty. Only the best I would see.

Many of us went down to the beach for a swim, carrying long candles to light the way. The water felt like silk as we dived beneath its folds. 'One of These Nights' by the Eagles drifted on the night air as we lay upon the cushions, telling stories and laughing. David and I strolled home hand in hand as the sun rose. The village was still asleep except for the morning song of the cockerel as the sun rose and the sound of the cats dashing behind the garbage bins as we passed. Random clinking of bottles could be heard in the distance as the deliverymen removed the crates from their vans.

The nights were so hot we were sleeping on mattresses in the courtyard. It was under the orange blossom our first child became a reality. During this pregnancy—in fact, all four—I felt so fulfilled. A warmth nurtured my heart as the feeling of our child grew inside.

Back home in England, David would make me cod and spinach crespaline, which I craved a lot. Each day in the spring, I felt the flowers' beauty when I walked in the garden and gathered the mulberries for making preserves. Thank goodness, while I was breastfeeding I had a daily craving for mulberries and custard with a Mackeson (stout beer rich in B vitamins). I did not drink during my pregnancies.

One evening there was a documentary about Leboyer, a French doctor and his method of childbirth. It held my attention so much that I had to find out more. This was way before Google, so it was a challenge to get more information. It certainly was not in my encyclopaedias. In addition, the idea of giving birth in water was rather revolutionary. This led to finding a doctor who would allow us to do it in a hospital. English health care in those days insisted that for your first delivery you MUST have it in the hospital! So doing it at home was out.

Even the thought of having my first baby at home was revolutionary for an average American girl from a working middle class family. Eventually, we did find a doctor at the West London Hospital who was practising the method. I regret that I have forgotten his name. He also told us about classes at the hospital called Lamaze, which is a form of breathing and relaxation for labour. David and I went to the classes to prepare for the day when Alice would enter the world. We were partners all the way.

The Floyd were finishing the recording of the *Animals* album at Britannia Row, so I was home a lot in the evenings. Emo was staying with us and was going through a rather unstable phase of his life. I had gone to bed early and could hear him crashing about downstairs.

The telly was blaring and so was he, with rather vile swearing. His moods were unpredictable at the time. I was extremely worried so I called David and asked if he could come home, which he did. I was in my later part of my pregnancy and I was very sensitive. I did not feel strong enough to confront Emo and tell him to shut up for fear of his reaction. I must add that Emo eventually found his Spiritual Master, Charan Singh, started to meditate and became the best friend one could ever have.

As it seems with most women, the day I was to go into labour, I took to washing all our sheets and blankets, as well as our clothes.

We had a washing line outside and I loved hanging my washing there. I loved the smell of the outdoors on our clothes and sheets. I had tons of energy, so I cleaned and washed the kitchen. We also went to the pub for dinner. I should have known my baby was coming, as the classes had advised us to look out for this behaviour.

We had decided to let life give us the surprise of whether it would be a boy or a girl. David and I had a list of names that we both agreed would be our choice. We decided to wait until we felt the soul of our baby and knew its gender as we held it in our arms before we chose its name. Though soul was not a term we were using then, I am sure our hearts worked that way.

On the evening of 7th May 1976, I went to bed, leaving David watching telly downstairs with another friend, Willie Wilson, who was the drummer in David's first band, Jokers Wild. Around 10pm, after my bath, I started to have weird sensations of energy rising and falling. They were not painful, but I decided to time them. They were coming quite regularly and frequently, so I leaned my head out of our bedroom door and asked David to come upstairs. We decided that we should make a move.

David grabbed my suitcase and his little bag with all the helpful essentials, as he was to be my labour partner. We drove into the night towards London. The streetlights were blinding, as the energy was getting stronger. With each corner, I found it more difficult to do my breathing techniques; I twisted, I turned and I whimpered. David held my hand gently as we drove through the streetlit night. It seemed like we were in suspended animation.

As we entered the hospital and went up the stairs, the experience became more intense. I felt like I was on LSD. I held my tummy as David guided me down the corridor. The lights were a surreal colour of green. Women and their husbands were walking slowly down the corridors moaning. It was like a Fellini movie. Finally, we reached the area where I needed prepping.

The staff separated David and me, as they assured us that it wouldn't be for long. Two wonderful Philippine women met me in a room that seemed like an operating room. They asked if I had had a bowel moment, which I had. They started to shave me as I kept asking if they had called my doctor. I pleaded, "Where is my husband?" I told them that we were to have a "Leboyer" birth in water and my husband was to be by my side. "*Please*," I cried, as the possibility of it all drifting away entered my mind.

The women giggled. They did not see the importance. It was all happening so quickly I had thoughts that I might just have my baby there with them. The energy waves seemed painful, but I was panicking. I was tense, as how we had intended our baby to be born might not happen. Finally, the nurse took me to another room where David, thankfully, was waiting. The sight of his long hair and loving attention calmed me down for a moment.

They laid me flat, which was not helpful. Gravity works against one in this position, so they lifted the back of the bed as I requested. I wish now I had known more about what helps labour to be easier, i.e. to be on all fours. David was setting out his things to help the contractions to ease. I remember he was betwixt doing that and holding my hand and trying to get someone to call our doctor.

The contractions were very strong, and the pace increased. I kept asking for my doctor. David kept trying to get him and at the same time stay by my side. There were noises coming from everywhere as the staff came in and out with metal tools and bowls. The tensions grew, upon reflection; it was becoming evident that our idea of our baby being born in the water was disappearing. I had to adapt, and I had to accept with grace what was to come.

The nurses kept asking, "How are your pains, dear?" This is not the way to help someone to be relaxed and do Lamaze. It was obvious that they had no idea. David and I were adrift in the normal obstetrics philosophy. I started to analyse the pains and was just about to give in to having an epidural when my doctor arrived and said, "The baby is coming! Breathe! Push!" It was sunrise. The birds were silent. It felt like all the world had stopped to listen and honour our baby being born. A rush of the most orgasmic feeling ran through my being when someone said, "It's a girl!" We laughed with our tears of joy. Silence captured the Beauty of that moment until she let out her first sound. David leaned over and stroked my face. Looking deep into my heart he said, "Shall we call her Alice?" I agreed. She was born on 8th May 1976, as the daylight filtered into the room. She was a sunrise baby full of Light.

England was having a hot spell and Alice came over with a rash. The nurses said that we had to stay longer to make sure all was well. Most of the women let their babies be taken away in the night and were given sleeping pills. I refused. I wanted to sleep with her next to me. The nurses said she was ill because I held her all the time. I said, "Nonsense, it was the heat and the blankets!" I continued and we eventually went home. Moreover, after getting home David and I had Alice sleeping between us for over six months.

During our pregnancy, I had read a book called *The Continuum Concept*, by Jean Liedloff. She was an American writer who had spent two and a half years deep in the South American jungle with stone age Indians. The experience demolished her Western preconceptions of how we should live. While reading it, I had the same reaction. This tribe related to each other and did not seem to have any of the psychoses that we have in our culture, and that inspired me. They carried their babies until they could crawl.

I bought one of those baby carriers, which enabled us to hold her against our chest, hearing our heartbeat. When I wasn't carrying her, David did. The only time she was let down was when she was sleeping next to us. I sang her sounds of love, and instinctive sounds of the heart. Later in life, I trained in healing harmonics, which are so similar. Sounds can so influence peace.

We had a dear friend and nurse, Rose Renwick, cooking and caring for us so that we could focus on bonding together as a family. She was a great cook! Rose was the wife of Tim Renwick, a fantastic guitarist, who has continued to work with David over the years. He too was from Cambridge and having Rose cook for us brought us even closer as friends. I will always be grateful for her care, because having one's first baby is such a learning curve; I didn't feel alone.

We were riding high on bliss until one day Alice came down with gastroenteritis. She cried and cried. We had a door that connected our bedroom to the next. We walked around from one room to the hallway and back again, sharing, trying to calm her down. Suddenly, the safety net of being in a hospital was not there and Rose was gone. The reality hit. What do we do? This was our first experience of being responsible for a wee one.

She was so precious, and our hearts were hurting. We were exhausted and seemed alone; however, we had to get through the night. We were so concerned about our precious child. Honestly, I must admit there was a moment as I was holding her in my arms, looking out into the night sky, exhausted, forlorn, I was so desperate for the screaming to stop.

The next morning, we took her bundled up in her blanket to the doctor. He said, "She's dehydrated and getting gastroenteritis." If it did not change, we would have to go back into the hospital. Life took a turn in that moment; the fear of losing our precious Alice seized our hearts. As it turned out, the liquid antibiotics and extra saline water from the chemist saved us.

The experience tarnished the height of joy we were feeling for me, but I cannot speak for David. I took a turn; depression set in, coupled with exhaustion. During that time, I never thought I could have another child. They called it post-natal depression and it certainly was a shock. Fortunately, Alice and David were the loves of my life and I made it through to find bliss again. Watching the beauty of their love grow was my medicine.

EARLY CHILDHOOD
DADDY HIDES US AWAY
USA 1954

I sat looking out from the leaded light windows of Woodley, holding little baby Alice close to my breast, feeding her. I pondered my own beginning. Memories of those early years in Philadelphia returned with the reality of now being a mom. As children, we would often play in the streets, playing tag with other children. In the summer, the city fire department would open the fire hydrants on the holiday weekends so that we could cool down and frolic in the water.

One particular morning, I had my toys out on the sidewalk and was pretending to cook dinner for my girlfriend, who lived next door. I didn't hear my mother calling me from inside despite the fact we always left our doors open in those days. "Charlie, Charlie come here!" Charlie was my name at home.

Suddenly, she came out from the house looking rather tense. "Charlie, did you not hear me?" she shouted. "Pick up your toys and get in here! Now! We are going to visit your Aunt Dot and DO NOT tell anyone!" My girlfriend had returned outside when she asked what I was doing. I tried not to answer for I was an extremely obedient child down to the letter. I bit my lip, but I could not keep the secret as her demands increased. I was only five years old.

The next thing I remember was my mother hustling my younger sister, Donna, and me out the door. Like little ducklings, we rushed down the street behind our mom trying to catch a cab to the train station, bags and all. Mom then bought the tickets and hurried us to the platform so as not to miss the train. It seemed exciting and yet unexpected. I loved Aunt Dot as we had visited her before. Daddy often drove us up to her house in Connecticut for the odd holiday.

It was a sunny day and I sat next to the window in the train feeling its warmth, daydreaming. Donna was sitting on Mom's lap. We had stopped at another station when I heard my father's voice: "Where do you think you are going?" He picked up Donna, yanking me with his other hand from where I sat. My mother was caught off guard. Everything happened so quickly; he was supposed to be at work. She grabbed my other hand as he dragged me across her lap.

I became the centre of a tug of war. All the other passengers gawked in suspended animation, wondering what was going on. All were shocked into silence and non-action. My mother lost her grip as he took us down the coach. I still can hear her feeble cry pleading to him, "Please don't take them. Please don't take them." We left the train just as the doors closed; it was over. Daddy hid us in the New Jersey countryside with his parents, in their newly built house. And I forgot that I had a mother.

Baking apple pie, rival cake and making jam filled the time with our grandparents. Nannan's kitchen was large, with a pine table in the centre. She was like the perfect image of a fairy godmother, bonnie, grey haired and with a smile that warmed your heart. Her apron was always covered with flour or some sauce she had been making for dinner. Her pantry was a child's delight, full of preserves, chutneys and jams. Herbs hung from the ceiling and filled the room with drifting fragrances, which held me spellbound each time I entered to fetch something for her.

PopPop, my grandfather, was a welder and worked from home in his garage. His white T-shirts were always covered with little holes from the sparks. He never shaved, and with his prickly beard, he chased and teased us without mercy. When he finally caught us, he would rub his whiskers across our faces as he held us in his arms. We squealed with glee as he continued to tickle us. It was such a fun game, which we played often in the gravel driveway.

My father's sister, Aunt Dolly, had two children, both boys, Tommy

(Butchie) and Billy, who came to live with us. Story has it that their father had wanted girls and my father had wanted boys so we all wound up and placed with our grandparents. It really didn't matter, because our grandparents showed us so much love.

Their house was like a fairyland haven for me. Nannan collected salt and pepper shakers which adorned her living room windowsill. She would often sit and crochet another doily or tablecloth in her big armchair by the window. She taught me how to do the same, and to knit. A grandfather clock hung on the wall; it was a family heirloom from the old country which had a cuckoo that cuckooed on the hour. PopPop would rewind it each evening by pulling the metal pinecones on the chains that dangled from the main part of the clock. Tick tock, tick tock echoed throughout the house.

Each morning Butchie, Billy and I would go out into the pinewoods and collect blueberries for our morning cornflakes. Donna was too young to go with us so she sat by the window with her head in her hands, grumpy until we returned. Donna and I wore the exact same crinoline dresses, which I found out years later were from our mother. She must have sent them to our old address in Philly for she did not know where we were. Dad must have passed them on to our grandparents secretly. They were so pretty.

One afternoon, as we were playing in the dust near the main house, a little powder blue car drove up the driveway. A man came out saying he was a "Fuller Brush man." Fuller Brush men were door-to-door salesmen in America selling merchandise for the home. My grandmother stood listening as we all gathered behind her skirt, seeking safety. PopPop was out on an errand and we were the only ones home. We were curious who this stranger was and listened from behind Nannan's skirts, peeking out occasionally.

Suddenly a woman with dark hair and eyes sat up from where she had been secretly lying on the back seat, out of sight. In almost the same motion, she opened the door and got out. My grandmother tensed as I ran out up to her. She was beautiful. I asked, "Who are YOU?"

She replied, "Why, Charlie, I am your mother."

"Oh, really? Would you like to come in and see my toys?" I asked as I grabbed her hand.

At that moment, my grandmother grabbed my other hand, shouting at my mother to go away while at the same time demanding that we all go inside. The Fuller Brush man called out to my mother, "Ginny, come on. We know where they are now." She let go of my hand reluctantly with tears in her eyes as she got back into the little blue car. Gran held me close, wrapping me safely in her arms, also with tears in her eyes. I was confused, but returned to play with the others as I watched the car disappear down the drive, leaving a trail of dust.

I have no idea how much time had passed before my dad's summons brought us to court. Daddy, Donna and I all went together. The building was amazing. It was huge, with marble floors and round pillars. There were rows and rows of wooden benches with people sitting on them. Daddy led us to one and asked us to sit down. As we waited, we could hear other names called in the distance, echoing around the room. We felt very tiny in such a place. I held Donna's hand tightly, hoping this would keep us safe from harm.

Before we arrived from the station, Daddy had said that we must not mention his friend Agnes. I think I was too young to understand or know if they were living together since we spent most of our time in the country. But that is what he asked.

Daddy stayed, while a nice lady escorted Donna and me out of the room. She held our hands and assured us that we would return soon. We walked across the white marble floors, our shoes clicking as we shuffled along until we came to a rather large door.

She knocked and waited for a voice to speak. "Come in," we heard from the other side. We felt even smaller as we entered the room as the ceiling was so high. All the walls were covered in wood and large shelves of books with gold letters. There were carpets in bright colours, a huge desk and large leather chairs. We both sat on one together with our feet dangling over the side. The kind lady left once she knew we were comfortable.

Across the room was a man who was wearing a black type of robe and a white collar. I suppose he was our judge, but I am sure we had no idea. What was a judge? He was just a man who had a pleasant voice and gentle eyes. We were there for a while and he asked us many questions. The only one that I can remember was "Does your dad have a girlfriend?" I froze, but Donna shook her head, her blonde bob moving with her gesture, as she said, "Yes, Agnes." Later, I was mad and kicked her, and said, "Daddy said we shouldn't tell anyone." Accompanied back to the courtroom, we found Daddy sitting on the bench looking rather forlorn. Three women with dark hair and eyes sat a few rows in front of us smiling and waving their hands. I recognised the one who said she was our mother. One of the other ladies was her sister, Dorothy (Aunt Dot) and the third was a close friend of theirs. (I remember her face, but not her name.) Beside them was the Fuller Brush man. In fact, he was Mom's lawyer and private investigator, Mr. Miller.

When we returned my dad stood up and the three women approached us. We stood at the end of the bench looking up at him with our blonde hair and innocent blue eyes, wondering what was going on. His voice cracked as he said, "Girls, the judge has decided that you both must go and live with your mother." We cried, and we fell into his legs, clutching them, me peeking to the side at those women. He continued to speak to our hearts as his fingers stroked our heads. "Please, girls, don't cry, for we shall be together every summer and I shall come to see you every holiday where you live." "NO! NO! Daddy," we pleaded.

The women got closer, and I looked at them again through my tears and the safety of my father's legs. I did not want to leave my Daddy and I had forgotten that I had a mother's love. These women were strangers. They pulled us away, holding our hands gently, to a path unknown. Trying to comfort us, my mother said, "Come, girls." I kept looking back as my father's waving image faded amongst the crowd. He went home to an empty house. We were gone.

We had to take a train to Connecticut, where my mother had a little house near my Aunt Dot. All the way, I sat alone behind them. They kept looking at me and smiling. Donna sat on their lap giggling. I was angry, sad, frightened and alone, not knowing that there was another surprise, a little brother, Stephen, waiting at home with my other Nan. We fell asleep in the taxi until they carried us into our new home.

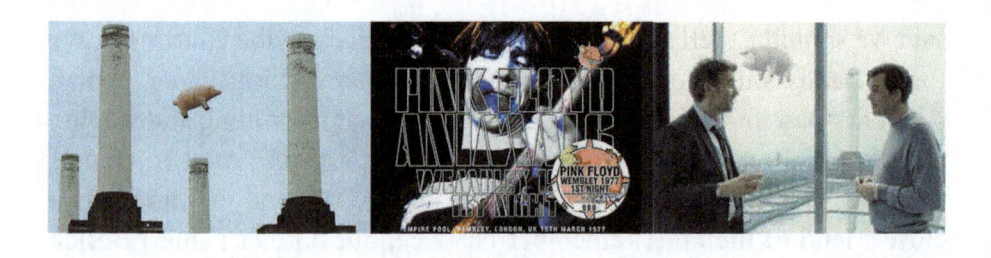

ANIMALS IN FLIGHT
BATTERSEA POWER STATION
DECEMBER 1976

It was early December, and the scheduled photography for the *Animals* album cover was to take place at the Battersea Power Station in London. The idea was to suspend a large inflatable pig called Algie between the four chimney stacks. Algie was 30 ft. long and full of helium, and the plan was to tether her within the middle of the antiquated building. For extra safety, there was a trained marksman on standby in the event she broke loose.

Apparently, Roger's daily drive to Britannia Row in Islington inspired the idea. He lived across the river, just off Clapham Common, and the station was a daily vision along the way. The image of the pig was born from the book *Animal Farm*, by George Orwell, as was the concept for the whole album. Storm Thorgerson, from Hipgnosis, worked together with Roger to design and execute his vision, which the rest of the band accepted.

The day arrived and we all gathered at the station to observe the photographing of the cover. However, the weather proved to be a bit inclement so the shoot had to be postponed. In addition, the cables were not secure enough to make it viable. The next day we arrived to try again, and despite the weather being a bit calmer, disaster happened. Algie broke loose.

The cable snapped and there was no marksman in sight. She shot up in the air, last reported heading for the English Channel. It made the news, with wonderful caricatures in the morning papers of two airline pilots looking out of the plane window, freaked to see a pig flying next to them. Was it a hallucination? They hadn't been drinking. Oh dear, it is a flying pig!

There was great concern that Algie would cause an accident in the air, but fortunately, she descended of her own accord. Thank God, for the winds had diverted the flight plan. The farmer whose field she came to rest in remained perplexed. There amongst the trees she hovered, bouncing gently before his eyes. He went back inside and made the phone call to the local police. "Hello, has anyone reported missing a 30 ft. long pig, have ya?" And the reply, "Are ya' sure ya' ain't had a pint, have ya? Ya sure it ain't a figment of yer' imagination?" "No, there really is a giant inflatable pig bouncin' around me field. I ain't jokin! Has no one reported a missin' pig?"

Word got back to the Floyd, who then sent Robbie Williams and few of the stage crew to the rescue. Their mission was to retrieve Algie safely. The famed mishap is amongst many fables in the Pink Floyd history books. Thenceforth, she and a few cousins became a regular feature in the *Animals* 'In the Flesh' tours. I even remember that during the *Animals* tour in the States one could find an isolated roadie backstage painting little baby ones. The idea would be to release them from Algie's behind over the audience. However, that never happened, or at least not to my knowledge.

When we returned home to Woodley, word had reached our neighbours, and what was a potential disaster turned out to be the local comical story of the week, or perhaps forever. To them it just added to all the animal adventures we had had over the years. It brought back memories of how Blu, our peacock, got away and the whole village was on alert trying to capture him, darting from tree to tree, field to field. Steve and Linda O'Rourke had given him to us for our wedding present with a message CLIP HIS WINGS. David didn't want to, and unknown to us peacocks could fly. Therefore the adventure began. He just flew out of our fenced chicken run into the sunset.

The Algie adventure brought back another animal memory of the time our neighbour's cow got into our garden. Puddy and I had just returned from shopping, and were greeted in the dark by a rather large cow. We tried to chase it back into the next-door field, flashing our coats, our metallic wellies we had just bought from Biba glittering in the moonlight. Poor cow, we must have been such a frightful sight. We were hooting and hollering like two crazy Halloween figures down the drive.

We were relieved the cow did make it home, but only after it jumped our five-bar gate like something out of a storybook. Stopping on a dime, its large body just missed the moving rush hour traffic, silhouetted by their lights in the dark. Puddy and I just stood there gasping, as she casually turned right, wandered down the road a bit, then turned into the field from whence she came. Phew, did we need a cup of tea after that one! We giggled at yet another animal adventure. Many more were to come.

PIGS ON THE ROAD
EUROPEAN TOUR
26–27 JANUARY 1977

The Pink Floyd story was out. Capital Radio's Nicky Horne had broadcast an epic documentary over the course of six weeks. Each programme was 45 minutes long and was the most all-embracing exposé of their vision and history to date. John Peel at the BBC jumped in and played the whole album, breaking the exclusive arrangements given to Nicky. *Animals* set the stage to awaken their slumbering public, but often it just brought criticism and conflict instead of enlightenment. Acceptance was not yet to come. It seems to be the way with all visions that challenge the status quo.

So the *Animals* tour began, and the first stop was Germany. The gigs were getting bigger and louder. In addition, as our families grew, our entourage became bigger also. Once again, our personal assistant Warwick McCreddie looked after us. We had Alice and our nanny, Jeannie, with us. We were getting to be dab hands at moving into hotels with a little one. Bed ready, bottles warmed and dinner was on its way.

After the first concert, with Alice safely in bed, David and I joined the others at a nightclub party which the promoters had set up. When we arrived there in a box was a live baby pig, shivering as the loud music surrounded him and the strobe lights revealed his form to us. The promoters thought that it would be funny. I freaked! The band told Warwick to take it back to the hotel and arrange for the farmer to pick it up as soon as possible, which meant taking him to his room at the hotel until it was resolved.

The next morning, Alice, Jeannie and I went down for breakfast and gathered as much lettuce, other vegetables, and bits of fruit as we could, knowing that Warwick would not have thought of that. We waited until we thought it was a reasonable hour to visit and see how the baby pig had fared. We were probably a bit early, but it was around 10am. Poor Warwick was extremely hungover and moaned as he opened the door. Suddenly he gasped and shouted, "OH MY GOD!" as he looked back into his room.

All the mirrors on the sliding wardrobe doors were cracked. The pig had been snorting at all the other pigs he could see and must have been kissing himself or had an argument to have created such damage. There was excrement everywhere. His room was literally a pigsty! As we looked around, we noticed that our little pink friend had dragged most of his straw out of the box on to the carpet, which Warwick had laid on its side. As he started to put back the straw, he came upon his underpants. The piglet obviously had slept with Warwick's underpants all night.

We didn't know whether to cry or laugh as the pig was running after Warwick as he tried to rescue his knickers. Alice loved the pig and wanted to feed him. We stayed for a little while until Jeannie shrieked and ran out of the door back to our room. She had forgotten that she was washing the nappies in the bidet and feared she had left the water running. I was against paper nappies then and we used cloth ones instead. It was a small attempt to save the trees. We washed them in the hotel bidet while on tour. When she got there, the water was running throughout the room and into the room downstairs as well.

We all left Steve O'Rourke to settle the situation. Between the pig's mess and ours, the hotel was not too happy. Another rock band destroys a hotel. Actually, the Floyd and their crew really had a good reputation. It was the pyrotechnics that caused a few problems, and of course the aeroplane. But I am foretelling a bit of the future.

THE BRIGHT SIDE IS CALLING
PARIS, FRANCE

In Frankfurt, the audience had been very violent. It was a certainty that within a cramped audience of 12,000 there would be a few nutters. In the first set, they took to throwing beer cans and other paraphernalia on stage. In fact, a bottle smashed on Nick Mason's Hokuszi painted drum kit, splattering him in the face.

There was a announcement during the interval asking them to stop as some of the delicate equipment was getting damaged. To add to the tension, the rented fog machines were not creating enough fog. They tried a smoke bomb machine instead. It worked too well. It released billowing clouds of smoke not only onto the stage but also into the audience, who could not see anything. The smell was so acrid that everyone's throat felt strangled and it made it difficult to sing. This did not go down well for David.

By this time, some of the flavour of the Beauty I found in the shows was wearing thin. I was getting a bit battle worn. Life on the road with a child and nanny, and struggling with my diet, was proving difficult. We travelled to city after city, from hotel to hotel. The Floyd were used to touring; yet, does one ever get used to it? There is a buzz mixed with the hardship of being away from home. I hear David's voice singing, "Home, home again, I like to be there when I can."

After five more gigs, we reached Paris, where the Floyd were to play at the Pavilion de Paris. Roger, David and I were in one of the cars, which was taking us to the gig. There was a drive to the back entrance that was about a block long, with a brick wall on the left and a high fence on the right, with only room for a car, not a limo. When we turned into the drive, there were fans waiting, lots of them, up to the gate. The driver went slowly into the crowd. There was nowhere for them to go, except on top of the car and squashed against each other, against the wall.

I started to laugh and laughed hysterically. Roger looked over to David and asked, "Why is she laughing?" David said, "That is what she does when she is extremely panicked." First, I laughed, because I could not believe what I was seeing, as the driver kept moving forward. Then, as it worsened, I laughed hysterically because my heart hurt at what I was seeing. They were screaming and banging on the car. Their faces were pressed against the windows. Their anxiety was a mixture of excitement that their stars were so close and OH MY GOD at being crushed. I wanted to get out, but there was no way to do so. I had to close my eyes and hold David's hand tightly. I found refuge against his shoulder until the nightmare was over.

This was just one of many experiences which the *Animals* tour seemed to attract. The album and the gigs portrayed this very aspect of our supposed modern culture and our inhumanity. The tour was a reflection of the sorrowful state of what was happening in the world. The topic played on the stage was also coming backstage. It was filtering into our home life. However, we continued, concert after concert with baby in tow. I often wondered what kept us going, but until the pus festers, a wound cannot heal, I suppose.

For me, the Beauty of those moments was when the audience and the music were one, which overshadowed the pain. But more rough seas were to come. I only wish that I could have helped David more, besides being by his side and raising our children. Reading some of their history now has opened my eyes more to understand what was going on with the band, often behind closed doors.

They were a gestalt in many ways, bonded together over the years. The band's inner relationships were torn yet entangled. This realisation time and time again appeared only after a crack started to emerge. What once was unity was now becoming shattered. Often the family was a refuge for each of them from the storm, but I wonder if it did not cause a schism in both camps. I believe it did. Our lives had become so big and surreal; or maybe perhaps unreal? For sure, it was beyond being a normal existence.

Things started to change. Roger's unending pain and anger placed a dark shadow over everything expressed in his lyrics. I have witnessed many times how the music made his anguish palatable. I saw how David's heart struggled to be heard and Rick retreated into silence, as if they were carrying a heavy stone. And somewhere amongst this turmoil of life, a creative force rose above the storm, touching our hearts out there, on the other side of the wall. Their music brought an archetypal message that one could rise above the challenges of life to find Beauty waiting.

Sometimes I wish I could go back in time and convey that message to them, not as a lovesick girl, but as me as a woman, who has found the value of Beauty. It wasn't the size of the shows. It was the mastery of being human through transforming ugliness into wonder and the Beauty of life. That is what their concerts created for us in the audience. That is what brought people back time and time again. Somehow, in revealing the shadows and the light we found balance, even if it was in the subconscious held in our memories.

They say that life only gives you what you can handle. Well, this was a big one. Much given, but with it came the burden we carried. Some days I just wonder, could it have been different? Maybe the path was laid before us that we were destined to walk. The tide was turning. The programme set. The bright side was calling us to go forward. Upon reflection it was a 'breaking-through' not a 'breaking-down', but it seemed we were the last to know.

FLOYD BECOMES CECIL DEMILLE
WEMBLEY EMPIRE POOL
1977

We had returned from Europe, with a few days at home before the Floyd's five gigs in the UK at the Wembley Empire Pool. David had contracted tonsillitis upon our return. Unlike in America, British children do not have their tonsils or adenoids removed. David would often have infections, but this time I presumed it started because of the earlier gigs in Germany. They had to substitute the dry ice with smoke and as a result, it entirely covered the stage, the band and the audience below. It was hard to breathe and dried out their throats. And who knows what else it affected.

When we got home, we took David to a specialist who worked with opera stars. His treatment was very effective, required a few visits and allowed David to sing. A special lozenge was the remedy, which was an essential in our home medicine cabinet for years. I remember even sending some to Paul McCartney, for which he was extremely grateful. He was struggling for his Wembley gigs at the time as well.

We left Alice at home with Warwick's sister Winsome and Peter Mount whom we considered our second family. We had bought a property on McGregor Rd, near Portobello Rd in London. There were three flats. We kept the top floor flat as a London bolt-hole. It was a sweet, one bedroom, modest flat arranged over three floors with a kitchen on the top floor. It was petite but very serviceable for weekends away. Emo was living on the first floor, and, of course, invited to all five shows. It turned out to be party time every night.

It was a relief to be back home with an English audience, for they were much more held, absorbing the music. It always seemed they allowed the notes to enter and dance around their being. Or were they stoned? More than 10,000 came each night and more hopefuls lingered outside, wishing they were there too. *The Financial Times* called the Floyd the modern day Cecil DeMille as *Animals* was more theatrical than ever before. The music floated from behind the inflatables as the show went on.

By the fourth night, I was feeling rather frail around the edges. I said to David, "I really can't do another late night." He agreed, but when we got home, Emo had invited everyone over and the party was in full swing. After a while I gave in and asked David if we had any coke. He said no, but he knew someone who did. He took me down to our bathroom where there were two ladies laying down lines. David asked if they would give me some for he had already had some a few moments before.

He left me there and went back to the party. I had a few and started back up the stairs to find him. As I passed our bedroom, I noticed he was lying there in the half-lit room with the door open. An energy of love took over, but as I came close, I felt I had to vomit. I ran to the window, which was half-open. Leaning out, I vomited into the night. I felt like my guts were being yanked out. My head was exploding. Finally, it stopped, and I lay down next to him.

I felt shaken but a type of euphoria was taking over. I asked David in a more intimate moment what it was that they had given me. He didn't know but it felt good. He hugged me and I fell asleep in his arms. Later I found out it was heroin! That was the last thing I would have EVER taken if I had known. It was a violation of my freedom of choice. Maybe they were unaware that I didn't know. And I didn't know that London was moving away from cocaine to snorting heroin.

From then on, I learned to ask more questions about what I was taking. That experience served to lay down the foundations to me quitting drugs. One good seed planted for the future and one bad seed put away and forgotten. For whenever something was too great of an emotional shock to face, I went into a form of amnesia. Just like I did when my father took us away from my mother. Mother? What mother? Heroin? What heroin? Life went on.

ANIMAL FARM COMES STATESIDE
IN THE FLESH TOUR, U.S.A.

The *Animals* tour started in Miami. The warmth of the balmy air was refreshing, as back home, April showers were preparing for spring. We had some time to swim in the ocean with Alice, as she loved the water. There were a few technical problems getting the pig to be present and it was suspended from a pole as a last minute solution. The highlight of the show was when the pig was set on fire, which was not quite what the crew had intended. Fortunately, they were on the case and no one was injured. However, it did set alight a few other fires, namely Roger's and Steve O'Rourke.

We flew everywhere in our private aeroplane, a 737 jet. Long gone were the times when we had to walk through airports, wait in lines, check in, and eat aeroplane food. Nope, not anymore. Our cars would drive up to a small terminal and our personal road manager organised our bags as we made ourselves comfortable inside. Life on the road had become a very complicated affair: families travelling with children and nannies, more equipment, friends, movie stars, fans surrounding us whenever they could find out where we were. We checked into hotels with aliases to ensure our privacy; that worked sometimes.

The gigs were becoming a blur as we travelled from state to state. The size of the lorries increased and so did the number of road crew. In the past I knew all their names. Now some were familiar while others were hired 'humpers.' The stadiums were so big that they needed strong Herculean men to get all their speakers up there. Nick referred to them as the 'quad squad,' the SAS of humpers. The organisation of the whole tour was a feat of great proportions.

As our journey took us through the south, I remember being amazed at what Americans thought was their architectural heritage. I say that because of what we saw when we went to see some of them, where their history supposedly happened. We visited one that was just a small pile of stones in the middle of the prairie. There was though a parking lot full of tourist buses, a gift shop and, by the way, they didn't fail to charge an entry fee. We left a bit cynical, remarking under our breath, "Perhaps we should tell them to go to Europe to know more of their heritage." But I do know, as an American, what we dream is as much a reality as a building.

Phoenix, Arizona was our favourite city to enjoy. We played in the desert with Land Rovers and went surfing in the artificial waves, and the Floyd had the best time driving madly on the circuit. There was time to frolic and sit in the motel jacuzzi. One of the most unforgettable memories was the morning when David drove a motorbike through the dining room for a bet. We were all having breakfast when Evil Knievel Gilmour came riding in from the outside terrace, passed our table, out the main door, through the lobby and out of the motel. He parked the bike and returned for breakfast. Nobody said a word. The waiters and all the diners just went on with their day. Business as usual seemed to be their motto.

We travelled like a pack, struggling sometimes to keep a smile covering our exhaustion and late nights and frivolity. The constant reminder of the growing conflict within the band took energy from us all. Maintaining anger takes a lot of energy, you know. We put on masks to hide the pain. We were becoming alienated, not only from the audience, with the band behind the headphones, but also from each other. Food on the road left us empty, with its non-dairy creamers and dried-up sandwiches in the dressing room. Tour catering was in its infancy, so for the crew it was burgers delivered. Bottles of Evian began to appear, and I am sure we were all dehydrated.

Finally, we reached California, where it was less like a conveyor belt of Joneses. Friends and family were appearing amongst the waves of the audience. At the time, the band was finding it a challenge to adjust to the large stadiums of nameless faces. Security and safety became more of an issue as the number reached beyond 80,000. I spent most of the concerts in the middle of them at the mixer. Often when the band felt they had had a bad gig, I discovered that I had a different impression, as I bounced into the dressing room full of joy. A cloud fell upon me as I went into the changed atmosphere. I recovered my composure and silently poured myself a drink.

On the first night at Anaheim Stadium, the start of the show began with a plane flying over the stadium with computerised lights on its belly blinking WELCOME PINK FLOYD. *Animals* had become more theatrical. The Floyd were mere puppets, it seemed, on the stage and in the distance. I admired this, for it gave an opportunity to listen instead of adulating upon our stars. Taken on a journey, because that was the Floyd they loved. Admittedly, I wished that there was less tragedy, less angst. It was as if Beauty had become a whisper. The music was just about audible amongst the props and the click track. It was not to David's liking nor Rick's as the click track took over.

One newspaper is quoted as saying: "The Floyd are something from a different century - rarely smiling, never speaking to their audience except to put down an unreceptive or maybe violent turbulence from below. Undeniably, they are good musicians with a unique style of composition, their main strength, and their claim to the kingship of psychedelia is their mastery of electronics. By employing quadrophonic sound in the round could seemingly place their sound effects anywhere in the theatre. This gave such a illusion of movement that anyone attending the concert on drugs most probably got a far bigger dose of psychedelia than bargained for."

It was Alice's first birthday on the 8th May and we gave her a party the day before because we had to get to the next gig on her real birthday. Many friends came to celebrate the day she was born in our hotel room. Cyndy Shirley and Aaron, her son, were a delight to share time together with as always. Over the years, we often took care of him at Woodley when Cyndy was away with Jerry, her husband, who was the drummer of Humble Pie. We felt he was our son in a way. We grew very close. Many years have passed and I have watched him grow up to be a fine man, husband and father. For me, they are still one of our extended families across the ocean.

I always marvel how backstage in California, especially in Los Angeles, it is like a film set of faces you think you know, but don't. People you see in movies or on telly become like friends, but you really don't know them. Madonna came one evening and received a rather curt comment from Roger, which shook her a bit. He was like that, he didn't play the Hollywood game, at least then. David continued to wear his jeans and T-shirts but succumbed later.

Fame is a weird paradox for me. On one hand, the artist loves what they are doing, wanting to be adored, wanting to be heard, but when it gets too large, in terms of numbers wanting you, it becomes a challenge. And perhaps it is hard even to know who you are amongst all the screaming voices in your head? So many people needing, feeding, depending, idolising can make it difficult to know who your friends are. And if the band you are in starts playing different tunes? What then? As I became more aware of my sensitivity as an empath, a healer and an artist, each time an album was announced there was a surge of psychic energy upon our home. One's life is taken over even when you sleep at night. Ah, but such is the path of a healer: feel, know and love.

SAVING THE HOGS
OAKLAND, CALIFORNIA

My sister Donna had flown in from Wyoming to see the show, but really, she came to see Alice and me. It had been a long time between visits. We went in our limousine to the gig. Both Dick Perry, saxophone player, and Snowy White, guitarist, came with us. It was special to share this aspect of my life with my sister. It felt like *Star Trek* as we went up the ramp and the metal gates lifted, allowing us to enter. My sister was casually dressed. I was wearing all white lace, but not for long. As we got out of the limo, I was appalled at what I saw.

Oakland Coliseum was a huge American venue with a large passageway that went completely around the building under the seats above. This passageway was wide enough for several cars and lorries to be there. We had entered just behind the stage, which made us feel very small in front of its majesty. However, to my surprise, there in that area was a pen filled with lots of hogs. Tied below their bellies were white canvas labels with each band member's name inscribed.

Along either side of the pen were ramps leading up on both sides with a thick long rope over the top reaching the floor. There were several very large men standing there as security guards. I approached them and asked, "What is this all about?" They laughed, placing their hands on their hips, and said, "Well, we are gonna whup the Floyd in a tug of war before the show!" The "we" was Billy Graham's team; he was the promoter, a very powerful promoter in the San Francisco Bay Area. They were big dudes and the thought of anyone falling onto these animals set me on fire. No way would this happen!

I asked Dick and Snowy if they had a pocketknife, which they did. I took it and in a swirl of white lace, I took flight. I jumped into the pen and started to remove the labels with the Floyd's names on them shouting, "I'll be damned if you will!" My sister stood there in awe of what was happening. Her angelic sister had become a tigress. I said to Snowy and Dick, "Go get Steve!" when one of Graham's roadies jumped into the pen and lifted me out, kicking. I then stood there addressing them rather forcefully, "How could you even think of doing such a thing! It's CRUEL!"

Steve eventually arrived and sorted it out, with some of the Floyd following. Fortunately, the farmer and his lorry were still there. I think he was hoping for a publicity shot because he wasn't too happy about being sent away. I have no idea what or if he was even paid. All I cared about was that it didn't happen. Later, someone told me that hogs could be very aggressive. I never felt that was the case. I think they knew that I was there to save them. I was their friend.

Ever since, I definitely knew I had an affinity with animals. I had become a vegetarian and with it I had an awareness of the plight of the animal kingdom. In fact, it has expanded to include the human kingdom and Mother Earth. In fact, before having children, I had a strong desire to have a wildlife park in the UK. I spent time looking for property and getting the information necessary to put it in place. I fell in love with white peacocks and other exotic animals. But with my deeper dream to have children with David blossoming, the dear animals had to wait except that night and others during the 'In the Flesh' tour.

TIME OFF IN PARADISE
KAUAI, HAWAII
MAY–JUNE 1977

The 'In the Flesh' tour came with a much needed and welcomed break: a month off between the middle of May and the middle of June was scheduled. Therefore, David, Alice and I went to Kauai in the Hawaiian Islands. As we landed in Lihue Airport and walked into the terminal, the Hawaiian women greeted us and placed their traditional Pikake Lei around our necks. The air filled with the scent of tropical flowers mixed with a warm touch of humidity. Immediately, my body relaxed, and a simple smile warmed my heart with joy. This was my first experience of Aloha as the land spoke to me with a deep feeling of coming home.

We had rented a condominium on the north shore in Hanalei Bay, approximately an hour's taxi journey away. As we drove down the island, we passed waterfalls and green jungle to find beaches hidden underneath trees sculpted by the winds. Alice and I looked out the window in wonder as the soft breeze blew her golden curls around her face. I held her hand as she pressed her face against the half opened window, jumping up and down on my lap and giggling.

The song "Puff the Magic Dragon lived by the sea, and frolicked in the autumn mist in a land called Hana Lei," by Peter, Paul & Mary, played in my head as we drove along the coast towards Hana Lei Bay. I wondered if they had been here too. It definitely was a time of magic. I felt so at one with each moment and rejoiced each day as Alice played in the sand next to David with triple rainbows overhead.

We often met up with Graham and Susan Nash of Crosby, Stills & Nash, who had a house there. I felt very at home with them for they had such heart. They collected shells from different beaches, which inspired me to begin my own collection. In fact, the children to this day bring me some as a present from their journeys around the world with their dad. During our stay, I remember getting up early to go to the beach, combing for shells with Billy, one of their friends, so that I could have a necklace made in the Hawaiian tradition. As it turned out, he made me a pair of large hair combs with shells and turquoise. I still have them safe in my jewellery box and every once in a while, I take them out to feel the sun and the ocean breeze of Kauai.

We fell so in love with the island that we nearly didn't return. There is a myth that the Goddess Pele, known for her creative power, passion, purpose, and profound love, will wrap you in the magic of Aloha if your hearts are pure. And if not, she spits you out, they say. Upon reflection, I am sure she was with us, making our stay a blessed one. She had us in the palm of her hand.

One day Graham told us of a special house that might be for sale. He hooked us up with the agent and at first sight, we were sold. It was a pyramidal shape on stilts, in the middle of a valley, with a stream running along the side. Although still under construction, we knew its potential. Paradise filled our being as we gazed out from the platform and listened to the sound of the clear crystal water rippling by.

There were avocado trees the size of oaks with plumeria and orchids in the underbrush. The unexpected sight of a red-crested cardinal totally took my breath away, for as a child this was a bird I loved. It turned out the homeowner was currently in jail, arrested on marijuana charges. We waited many years wondering if he would ever sell. Unfortunately, that day never came.

During our month stay, we heard of an old Hawaiian trail that linked the north and the south shore. Many people went on walks and camping trips into the jungle along that trail. There was nothing but nature: no restaurants, no electricity, no smoothie bars. David and I decided to go. He carried Alice in our baby sling on the front of his chest and I carried our minimal supplies for the day. We set off early so we could get back in time for sunset, as we did not plan to stay the night on the beach with a wee one unprepared. We walked and walked in the rising sun. There were flowers everywhere and running streams that we had to traverse. It was Beauty at our fingertips. The growing friction of the Floyd was left far behind.

Graham told us that we should try washing with the ginger shampoo which we would find along the way. They resembled red pinecones at the end of a stick of green leaves. Their cones are full of water and if you squeeze them, a clear, slimy-sudsy, ginger scented fluid comes out. The indigenous people still use the plant to wash, and to condition their hair and skin. So we had a go. It was slimy for sure.

Along the way there were walkers going back in the opposite direction. They asked how long we had been in. "A few hours," we replied. LOL. It seems that many stay there for months. Eventually we got to a beach and it was time for Alice to eat. We have the best photo of the moment when she dropped her carrot stick in the sand and proceeded to eat it. She spit and spluttered, passing it to me as I rescued her from her dilemma. We played on the edge of the waves for there was an undertow which made it difficult to swim, especially with a toddler.

The trail was full of colourful people seeking time out from the spinning world they had left behind. Each found their own refuge within the Beauty of the tropical jungle. And we, too, found our refuge in the tropical jungle—quite opposite from the jungle of rock 'n' roll. We were able to relax and laugh again.

Just before we left, we went to a kiddie birthday party. We found the house hidden away off the main road under the trees.

There were many children dressed in floating outfits of different colours, barefoot and tan. What was most remarkable was the stillness in their sounds of laughter and joyful play. It touched me very deeply. I saw that life could be different and wanted this for our family.

While on the island, it was easy to eat healthy and organic food. There were fresh fruit smoothie huts on almost every corner. In addition, the essence of Kauai empowered the vision that life was sacred and beautiful. The Oneness of Life was there. We felt the unity amongst men and nature—paradise on Earth. Even the fresh pineapples were divine.

This holiday planted another seed, which later would bring an inner change for me. When we returned to the road, I decided to stop participating in mood enhancers, including alcohol. This put me in a different camp. I was an outsider (at least that is how I felt). No longer did I go to the ladies' room for a smoke or a line. No longer did I mingle with the same high or take part in the same conversations. Another aspect of alienation crept into my life on the road.

The tension was growing backstage as Roger grew more unsettled. He was finding it more and more difficult to bridge the growing gap between him and the audience below. He was even finding it more and more difficult to continue to work creatively with the band as before. And as the days passed, it became more obvious.

As I relive those moments, writing, I feel Roger had a deep inner vision trying to get out. Perhaps it was his soul calling him. Perhaps it was his paradisiacal heart. Everything seemed a conflict, a confrontation. It was evident that he had to make a choice, which was challenging him down to his bones. Anger and frustration were often his way to deal with it. And it would continue that way until he resolved his inner turmoil. Again, quiet desperation was the English way, as we were unconsciously drawn deeper into the entanglement. Or perhaps not so quiet.

CHICAGO, CHICAGO
SUPER BOWL, SOLDIER FIELD
19 JUNE 1977

Playing larger stadiums, especially in the States, brought new challenges. At these concerts the audiences were let in earlier due to parking needs and the sheer size of the audience which could be up to 80,000 at some events. As the Floyd never had a support band, for various reasons, this meant there was nothing to amuse them. Plus, the weather was an added challenge, caught between baking sun exposure and/or rain. The crowd did get restless. Some got drunk and passed out. It was different from outdoor concerts in England, when the audiences would bring a picnic; Americans succumbed to the hamburgers, French fries and Coca Cola at the concession stands. Meanwhile it was a learning curve for the band, becoming conscious of crowd control, security and the safety of so many people.

On the *Animals* tour in the States the weather did prove a challenge, what with so much delicate equipment and never knowing when it might rain. A solution was found. From under the stage mechanical pale cream umbrellas would rise and open like flowers. It was magical! Suddenly we were transported to a French café in St Germain, Paris. They would catch the rain and it would flow down the centre support tube to the ground. It is rumoured that David didn't approve.

Many felt during these shows they were distracted by the Floyd's trappings. But at the same time the precision of their musicianship was astounding. In a way, the audience was guided away from focusing on the musicians into a metaphysical experience instead of a rock show. This was becoming their signature way of presenting their music. The visuals, the theatre, the concept merged together with the music. Having said that, it was a bit of a paradox as the topic of the songs emphasised a concern about mechanisation and the technological obsession of our culture. Hmmm? 'Welcome to the Machine'! I do wonder. Have we lost our humanity behind the box of illusions? Like the painter Goya, perhaps the Floyd's destiny was to wake us up from our slumber?

Steve had his hands full at the Chicago gig for two reasons. He had to deal with the unions. The Floyd had to have an extra union person for every crew member. I may be wrong but I believe in the end it was resolved with a payoff. The show was so complex and all the crew were specially trained. Union guys would not be up to scratch. Fortunately, they just stood there while our guys ran the show with no interference.

His other challenge was sorting the discrepancy of the official box office figure showing an attendance of about 67,000. He and the band doubted the accuracy and hired a helicopter, with a photographer on board to carry out a head count. They were right. The aerial estimate was around 95,000, which meant a shortfall in the takings of several hundred thousand dollars. Consequently, a Federal Grand Jury investigated allegations of mail fraud, wire fraud, kickbacks and other financial irregularities connected with this concert. Fortunately, the gig went well despite the unions and the mafia.

A WORLD SERIES ROCK 'N' ROLL SHOW
CLEVELAND, OHIO
25 JUNE 1977

The band was playing to bigger and bigger audiences. Their 'In the Flesh' gig in Cleveland has gone down in the *Guinness Book of Records* as one of the largest rock 'n' roll concerts in history. It certainly is one that has stayed in my memory as a testimony of how Beauty can arise out of chaos. That from the mire of sweat and tears something special can become.

The day was hot and sunny. We took our little Alice with us during the sound check. She had just turned one in May and was learning to walk. We took many photos of her toddling in the middle of the field in her little red and white polka-dot summer dress with matching pantaloons, her nappy peeking out the side. Occasionally she would teeter and fall over with a giggle. She was such a happy little thing.

As she grew older, she was like David's shadow, following along after him. Whenever I think of this time, the song lyrics from 'Me and My Shadow' come to mind. I just loved the bond she had with him even when she was a baby. My favourite photo was when she was bending over touching her toes with the inflatables behind floating above the stage. The contrast between her dinky innocence standing in the middle of this enormous patch of green and the majesty of the stage was special and yet surreal.

Crowds were building up outside the stadium. We could hear them getting a bit impatient in the sweltering heat, exposed to the blazing sun, squashed up against each other. Some had waited for seven hours. Some had stayed overnight. I heard later that it had been one confrontation after another between the cops and the punters. (Ohio had passed a decriminalisation law the previous year, so they couldn't bust anybody). Instead, they walked amongst them, harassing one person after another who was smoking weed, grabbing the bag of marijuana and dumping it on the ground. How appropriate the theme of the concert was in addressing this situation.

Time and time again the politically charged concept of *Animals* shocked the world. It was a musical take on George Orwell's novel *Animal Farm*. We were confronted with images and music that spoke of the corruption and social injustice that was prevalent, pigs, dogs and sheep symbolising the aristocracy, military and working classes respectively.

I had decided to sit at the mixer in the middle of the crowd that evening. Normally, the mixer area sat at ground level, but tonight it was raised up high. David suggested that I had better make my way out there before the audience arrived. Mark Brickman showed me the way, as he had to be there at lighting control. We went early and I waited for the show to begin with all the engineers and the setting sun.

Unfortunately, when the gates opened, the tension came into the stadium. Apart from the seats on the side of the stadium, the gig was what they called general admission, which meant that everyone had to find himself a spot on the grass. As the audience came in it was evident that a lot of them had had a gruelling day, waiting for hours in the sun to see the concert.

Reports vary. Somewhere between 83,000 - 93,000 people came to this show. They came to see a 'world series of rock show,' as described by a fan. They scrambled in desperation to get a spot, pushing each other aside. The smell of beer and reefer was in the air. The anticipation, mixed with frustration, became very noticeable as we were beginning to be surrounded, close up and personal with them, at the mixer. At one point, I was concerned that they might just push the platform over in their stupor, as some were getting a bit aggressive and out of control.

Sadly, someone let go of a smoke bomb into the crowd. Swirling lights of the ambulance in the distance held our attention. I really couldn't understand how anyone could do that at a concert meant to feel Beauty and wisdom. It might have hurt someone and did. Where had all the love and peace gone? My own fears started to build, as I could not escape. Everyone was counting the minutes until dusk when the concert would start at 8.30pm.

At the back of the stage were large signs of advertisements for Marlboro, Coca Cola and Winston. The sun was setting and from a distance in the sky came flashing lights towards us. It was our tour plane. This was even a surprise for me. The pilot broke the federal air safety regulations and flew right over the stadium at 500 ft. The sound and the unexpected rush that occurred when it flew over us shocked the audience into silence. Thank God.

The colours of the day began to fade into the night and became subtle hues of lilac blue as 'Sheep' began to gently fill the stadium. The sounds of 'Grand Chester Meadows' and the ringing of church bells took us on a Sunday walk in the English countryside at dusk. Then from the stage came puffs of smoke, adding to the ambience of the early morning mist, which carried out into the night twilight on the evening breeze. The crowd settled and were held in its wonder. One after another, what seemed to be puffs of smoke filled the air to open like miniature parachutes in the form of sheep.

For me this has to be my favourite concert ever! It exemplified how the Floyd could transform chaos into Beauty, and in that moment, it united us all. The album's theme was mainly 'Sheep' (people) followed into 'Dogs' (police) and then into 'Pigs' (masters/politicians) inspired by George Orwell's book *Animal Farm*. I had read the book during college and it was one that got me thinking deeply when I first read it. It was interesting to see how the Floyd interpreted it.

The evening faithfully followed through the story created. It was dark by now and the stillness of the evening took over as we were all further carried into the drama of *Animals*. I could relax for a moment and sat down, allowing myself to take in the music and the sound of David's guitar. During 'Dogs', large inflatables began to appear above the band in the shapes of the great American nuclear family - mother, father and 2.5 children - and all our toys: telly, a Cadillac, a fridge with phallic sausages hanging out. They deflated right on cue as all sang the lyrics we knew so well.

This tour of *Animals* required a huge amount of precision and timing. Roger was particularly demanding about getting the cues right and actually made a comment in his terse way that night over the PA, which got the crew scurrying around in a panic. A large inflatable pig appeared and went across the whole stadium. For me, he was one of the most menacing ones that they had created. At one point the pig got stuck over the middle of the crowd. An announcer came on and asked, "If anyone has hold of the line of the pig, please let go. It is very dangerous. We are trying to bring it back in from over the audience. Please, please let go of the line."

Despite it all, it was a 'world series of rock show!' But it was not so for the band. When I finally got backstage, there were just arguments and tension. Roger was not happy. He even treated the band as though they were hired hands. The tick, tick of the click track and the cues took over more and more. Many times, I have felt that they had no idea how special, magical and full of Beauty the gigs were they had created. Even in the mistakes, even with the click track Beauty did transcend. For them, I suppose it got lost in the details of their own isolated experiences. I am glad I had the memory of what they had achieved, along with many others. Oneness was often created within the audience as the band transformed the stress, alienation, and creative challenge of coming together for us all. It wasn't always 'Us and Them.'

Ultimately, even as we find ourselves in the current political, environmental, and economic turmoil, with many on both sides taking to the streets in order to make their voices heard, it's hard to not find similarities between Pink Floyd's message and today's current events. Though *Animals* certainly depicts a darker reality, the parallels are almost overwhelming. Let's hope we can ultimately wake up and work together to create a stronger future for everyone.

A REUNION OF FAMILY
PHILADELPHIA
JUNE 1977

We stayed in New York and travelled down for the gigs at the Spectrum in Philadelphia. My dad and step-mum, Agnes, lived in Philly on the north side of town so we took our limousine to pay a visit. They hadn't seen Alice or even a Floyd show so it made their day when we arrived in our limo. Agnes recently told me that over the years Daddy never knew who the DJ Gilmour was that he was always posting my pressies and letters to in England. Until one day, I had sent him a signed album from the entire band. "Pink Floyd, what in the devil is that?" he exclaimed. "What is she getting into now?" That was in the beginning. He eventually showed the album to some of the neighbourhood kids who exclaimed, "He's FAMOUS, Chuck!"

Agnes said that my father's chest grew bigger and bigger with pride as the realisation dawned. He was ever so popular with all the local children and even more so once they knew who his daughter was married to. So on the day we arrived they all appeared as our stretch limo came up in front of their house on Kirby Drive. Albums and pens in hand, they were hoping to meet their idol. However, they had to wait, as David would come the next day. Apparently, Daddy had no idea what was happening, but Agnes said he loved it.

There was also a family gathering in the custom of the 'Hasenbeins.' Uncle Tom, Aunt Marie and Aunt Anna arrived, including Agnes' mom, Elsie. Nannan and PopPop were still alive and made a special trip from New Jersey to see us as well. It was the last time that I saw them all for they passed over in the following years. It was a great and lovely reunion with that side of my family from childhood.

Many summers as a child were spent walking the boardwalk in Wildwood, New Jersey with them. Uncle Tom especially used to spoil us with lots of cotton candy and funny jokes. The summer evenings were balmy with the sound of children squealing as they twirled on the rides above the crashing waves below. Aunt Anna and Aunt Marie and Elsie loved all the games, which there were lots of to place a few pennies on. The ding ding still plays in my ears as a tourist won their stuffed toy.

In our recent phone conversation, Agnes told me that Wildwood was always a place they came during the Great Depression of her childhood. Their home was just on the Frankford Junction, which had a direct line to Wildwood. Her family often would hop on the train for a day out to walk on the boardwalk. Later, when the family could afford it, they went by car. Listening to her brought back so many memories for her and for me.

David came the next day, but had to leave early for sound check and we were to meet him at the gig later. Agnes recalls that David was extremely warm and gracious to them. In fact, she says that all her Pink Floyd memories were joyful and everyone they met was warm and gracious. She chuckled last night as she remembered their first concert. She said, "It was really exciting!" A rock concert was never something either of them would have ever dreamt to experience. She was surprised how much she enjoyed it. I could see the sparkle in her eyes from her voice. Gee, I am so glad to have asked her now. She said, "It was loud!" with a chuckle. In addition, she was amazed how much everyone enjoyed the music. "AND they knew all the lyrics!" she exclaimed. Their attention fascinated her. And my dad was chuffed how popular he was with the people he sat next to, once they knew he was family.

As Daddy and Agnes got ready, I had the limo driver take Elsie, Uncle Tom and my two aunts home. Agnes will never forget the look on their faces as they drove away, which was their first limo ride. They felt royal. And I shall never forget the smiles upon my dad's and Agnes's faces when they saw the neighbourhood children standing on the sidewalk saluting as we left the drive.

I don't recall much about the concert as they were beginning to be one and the same. Looking after a child on the road took more precedence, which at least added a flavour of humanity within the blur, ensuring that we didn't lose touch completely with daily life. Having said that, it was still special (though taxing), as the hours were long. Early mornings, even with a nanny, travelling with a private plane, unpacking, packing, hotel after hotel, food on the road, the gig and the late nights were not quite what I thought the path of love and motherhood would be.

However, as I have often said, there was something that made all of that ok—between the travelling, the gigs, the groupies, the alcohol, the sleeping pills, the uppers, and sometimes cocaine. We were a mule train linked together by a common experience. Somewhere amidst the chaos there was Beauty and hope, which kept us going. Perhaps it was the music or the Beauty uniting us all. We just kept those doggies rollin'!

A PARADE OF ANIMALS
NEW YORK CITY
1–4 JULY 1977

Next stop was New York, New York and it was over the Fourth of July weekend at Madison Square Garden. This would be the first time for the Floyd to perform at MSG and we heard that Columbia Records had staged a publicity stunt to promote the album. Apparently, they paraded live animals up 6th Avenue to Central Park behind a flatbed truck bearing a video camera and loudspeakers blaring the album. A few of Columbia's personnel walked behind with a pig, a sheep, and a dog, along with a hundred or more fans. Quite a stunt. Poor animals; but who are the animals really, I wonder? I am glad I was not there to see it. I might have thrown up a fuss.

As we entered Madison Square Garden for rehearsals, I could feel its history within its walls. This place was where Marilyn Monroe sang "Happy Birthday, Mr. President." It was JFK's 45th birthday celebration on 19 May 1962, and I was thirteen. It was a special day for America to celebrate, the day the president was born. He was a president we loved. I remember just how much it meant to me as I watched it on the telly with my family. It is so powerful when a nation is held in honour together. It reaches beyond the telly. It touched my childhood heart that night with love.

More memories emerged as I sat in the empty hall listening to David warming up. Roger walked back and forth across the stage giving directions to the road crew. Things must be right. It was here that John Lennon made his final live performance. It was 28th November 1974. Elton John was in concert, when Lennon walked onto the stage. The audience was silent as the surprise took hold. They had made a bet while recording 'Whatever Gets You Through the Night.' If it made it to number one, Lennon would join Elton in his Thanksgiving Concert, and it did.

He lived up to the deal and rocked out together with Elton on stage. They also sang 'Lucy in the Sky with Diamonds', which further filled the hearts of the audience with joy and the feeling of miracles. With arms swaying in the air, the magic of the song came alive once again. Now it was our turn and it was another national celebration, 4th of July, Independence Day for the USA.

Juliette Wright and her children, Gala and Jamie, were to fly in from London for the shows. I was looking forward to spending time with them for we had become good friends ever since I arrived in the UK. I had spent a lot of time with Rick and Juliette in their London home watching their children grow up. Juliette was highly cosmopolitan and I met many creative and eccentric people who I found very inspiring. We always had a laugh, and I can still hear the sound of Juliette's mirth, as we often sat together at the mixer.

During our time together, Rick and Juliette shared many stories about the early Pink Floyd, especially about Syd. It was all new to me. I had been carried like a feather on the wind into their history. I wanted to know more. Rick had been very close to Syd, trying hard to help him find balance towards the end of his time with the band. One of Syd's girlfriends, Lynsey, would often be there at their dinner parties or just over for a cup of tea with the girls for a chat. She was so beautiful and reminded me a bit of Jayne Mansfield.

Lynsey and I often spent time together walking down the King's Road, window shopping, appreciating all the London fashions. We had stopped in a café for a light lunch when she shared with me that Syd was a real challenge, as he was prone to being jealous. Their relationship was during the most difficult period, when Syd was becoming rather unstable. He was possessive, controlling and prone to explosions.

I can see why he was that way due to his insecure and drug-induced perspective. It seems he had reoccurring concerns about the loss of his relationship with her. His insecurity was stirred by the fact that she was extremely glamorous, and men were very attracted to her. She loved him. His concern was unfounded but was real to him. As he was not of sound mind at the time, this characteristic rather dominated their relationship, which had to end, sadly, to safeguard her own sanity. Rick once said, "Syd clearly was never going to come back!"

I hadn't been in the States during the 4th of July celebrations for many years, let alone in New York for a Floyd gig at Madison Square Garden. There was such a buzz in the air as the essence of independence marked the moment. American flags came out of the closets and were waving in the breeze, hanging from the apartment buildings and windows. Huge flags were on metal poles everywhere. People were wearing red, white and blue everything. It was a party in the streets. My heart filled with such happiness at being home once again in America in this atmosphere of jubilation.

I loved Europe, but 4th of July weekend awakened something archetypal as I looked out of my taxi window. It was my national spirit. On that day, Juliette, Jenny McCredie and I were going shopping, which was our custom when arriving in NYC. We always looked for something that was special and not found in London to take home. Jenny was the wife of Warwick, who was one of the first of David's friends that I had met way back when my journey began. They were part of my family across the waters. Now Warwick was our PA on tour and his sister, Winsome, and her husband, Peter, took care of our home and animals. Later they became surrogate aunt and uncle for our children.

The Floyd were always punctual. Their gigs started at 8pm sharp and on this night the audiences were hyped up and ready. Tickets were hard to get, as they had to be purchased by mail order, so it was a precious evening for most. When the lights dimmed, the crowd went crazy with whistles and shouts of excitement. It was deafening, but you could still hear the music. It was during 'Dogs' that the audience were taken to greater heights. David's guitar leads proved the best in the first half while the inflatables floated to the ceiling. The second half was oldies but goodies with 'Us and Them' holding the audience silently spellbound. But 'Money' as the encore got them to their feet again.

On the 3rd of July, the audience were more restless. It was getting closer to the 4th of July and the city, perhaps the country, was getting rather over-stimulated. In addition, marijuana had been decriminalised in New York State so a lot of the punters arrived stoned. Consequently, many had brought fireworks to the Garden. Many who sat up in the upper tiers set them off even before the concert began, throwing them into the seats below, and setting fire to the T-shirt of someone who was seated about five rows from the stage. Roger was on edge and not too happy about the tension that was growing. He shouted, "You stupid MOTHER-FU**ERS!" He further bellowed, "And anyone else in here with fireworks can just f**k off and let us get on with it!" This did alarm the band, the promoter and the NYPD, so much so that on the 4th there would be stronger precautions and searches at the door.

Fireworks were not to be the only challenge in MSG during our time in NYC. The local union insisted on doing our lighting. Ugh! The show was so dependent on its precision. There were so many elements to coordinate that only the band's trained team could do it. This was not the first time there was an issue with the unions. Steve O'Rourke was on call, trying to find a compromise. Roger swore at them at the end of the show for their incompetence and inability to work together. Fortunately, the fans did not seem to notice. They loved the gig. The show went on despite the pops and the bangs.

On the morning of the 4th, I had the idea to take a horse drawn carriage from Central Park to the gig. Juliette and Jenny were up for it, though I did have to work hard to inspire them. We were dressed in our usual New York City finery and embarked upon our adventure in the open carriage. Rick and Juliette's son, Jamie, sat up front with the driver, exuberant as a young boy would be. It was super riding down the Manhattan streets and the weather was perfect. My favourite movie clips of couples in love, circling Central Park, sparked my imagination, as we rode along under the leaves of the trees. I just loved NYC.

As we got closer to the venue, the crowds started to build up towards the entrance. The NYPD were performing searches for fireworks and other unacceptable items. Of course! I hadn't thought about this situation the night before. Crowd control was keeping the tension checked. At least, we hoped. Unfortunately, it became more difficult to penetrate the crowd with our carriage. We found ourselves stuck amongst them, feeling a bit vulnerable as their agitation grew. They were packed like sardines in the heat, worried they would miss the start of the show. Some started to whistle and make wise cracks as we inched along. The horse got nervous along with us. Gone was the security of our limousine. Our eyes reflected our concern behind a brave face and a smile.

We finally reached the backstage entrance all a tremble, still in the carriage, for we were too frightened to leave it amongst the crowd. Juliette and I both agreed that never again would we let our hearts' fantasy put us in such a situation. We were just grateful to have got to the gig safe and in one piece. I often wonder how the journey home was for the carriage man and his horse.

I sat at the mixer as usual, but could not stay long as my nerves were a bit shot. The audience seemed so on edge it sparked mine further. The mischief the night before and our carriage experience left me unsettled. Feeling the fervour in the hall, being between excitement and frustration, became too much. So I left to find sanctuary backstage. Brian Humphries, their sound engineer, told me later that just minutes after I had left, a mini firecracker exploded close to where I had sat. The one firecracker that got away, eh? What grace that was. Time and time again, I have been protected even from my own folly.

IS THERE ANYONE LISTENING?
MONTREAL
6 JULY 1977

It was during the latter part of the tour that the sizes of the crowds were getting Roger down. In fact, in Montreal, he actually spat at the audience because he felt that they were only there to party and not to listen. I have to agree with him up to a point. Sitting out at the mixer gave a different perspective. Most of the audience was there to listen and did. The unruly ones up front made most of the commotion. During the recording of *Animals*, Roger started to act as if he was the sole writer and master of ideas for the band. In addition, he was the only reason that the band could keep going. Gone were the days of unity with the *Dark Side of the Moon*. He was starting to treat the others as hired musicians, sadly, forgetting how the Floyd came to be.

I always saw Roger's frustration, but he was becoming more narcissistic. I firmly felt that he did not realise the energetic and creative parts that David and the others contributed towards balancing his character traits. Or realise how much they were a gestalt and that their music formed through their alchemical process. It might just be his soul, calling him to leave the band. He was a tortured man. Our challenge was not to go down the slippery slope with him. Time would tell.

Roger had divorced Judy, his first wife, in 1975 and had fallen in love with Lady Caroline Christie. They married in 1976. Their bond seemed to reinforce Roger's ego trip or perhaps encouraged his path of his own creative realisation. The process did stir the waters. All the wives stood behind their man but each had a different way of doing that. As the families grew, the gestalt of the Floyd had to adapt. Whether that was good or not, it was what it was. Roger was always taking a lot of his frustrations out on Rick and I slowly observed Rick's resolve breaking over the years. Somehow, I don't think he liked being a punching bag. Who would?

We were in France, and some of us had rented a home while the Floyd recorded their next album, *The Wall*. On one occasion we were all having lunch at Roger's house, sitting by the pool. Each of them had been gifted Cartier watches. Roger was in one of his moods when he asked if he could look at Rick's watch. As Roger was holding it in his hand, he leaned over the pool and dropped it in the water. Rick said nothing. The expression on Roger's face was one of silent satisfaction. He had won that round.

I think, on that day, I began to lose my tolerance for the psychological games they often played between each other for fun. David often stayed quiet and even today his guitar is where he expresses the depth of what he feels. Unfortunately, our life together was changing, as the music changed its emphasis into transforming Roger's archetypical struggles. Or were they ours as well?

At that last gig in Montreal, David had held a silent, stubborn stance and walked off the stage because the band did not perform well. He refused to do an encore because he felt it was a lie of honour. The gigs were getting so technical. The music was becoming lost in the tension. He used to be in his creative world, sometimes standing with his back to the audience, feeling. Now he had headphones. They all had headphones. And the freedom to feel the music was disappearing behind the click track.

This was the night that Roger lost his temper and spat at one of the obnoxious punters below. It was a huge stadium with a sea of faces before them. Across the air there was a very sweet, tangible smell of reefers and cheap wine. Unfortunately, there was also a small group in the front rows, close to the stage, obviously high and rowdy. They were loud and the band lost their ability to sense the crowd. At one point Roger lost his patience, caught the attention of one of the loudest shouting and spat at him.

Over the years, for the final encore of the last gig on a tour, the Floyd always played a slow twelve-bar blues while the crew slowly removed the equipment and instruments. The intention was that there would be one lonely musician to walk off stage. A closure for a job well done.

But Roger was not alone in feeling depressed about this situation and on this occasion David had had enough. He was greatly upset by the mood of the concert and walked off stage. He refused to participate in the final encore. Snowy White, the second guitarist hired as background support, had to take over. In fact, David went out to the mixer to access the situation.

My heart leaped to see him standing there. I didn't know what to do, hug him or hold my distance. I chose to wait, for I felt a storm brewing. Snowy remembers the moment that he was finally in the freedom of his guitar when the road crew without warning started to dismantle the gear. He had no idea about this end-of-gig ritual and continued to play until it was evident he had to leave the stage.

We returned to the UK exhausted and needing a break from that part of our life. But such a gift was not forthcoming. One morning, I awoke paralysed in pain from the waist down. I pleaded with David to contact Dr. Sharma. During the tour, Pauline White, Snowy's wife, had told me of him and recommended him highly. I had no idea why I wanted to see him. I just did. Later, I was to find out that Dr. Sharma was not only an orthodox trained doctor, but also was an Ayurvedic, homeopath and naturopath (all alternative healing methods). Of course, in those days I had no idea what that meant. I only knew that Pauline said he was brilliant! David found him and arranged an appointment immediately, but he first took me to an osteopath whose treatment eased the pain enough to get to London.

Dr. Sharma's practice was in Seymour Place, London. He was from India and in his office hung a painting of Ramana Maharishi, his guru. He took my pulses and looking at us from behind his glasses and white beard he said, "She should go to my private naturopathic hospital, Ludshott Manor. IMMEDIATELY!" This was located in the Surrey countryside. My time there was to be an experience that opened a doorway to my higher self, my path to God. To realise that such a thing existed was enough to cope with at that stage.

Dr. Sharma put me onto a diet of grapefruit and chamomile tea and introduced other therapies that were extremely new to me. In addition, I was not to have any contact with the outside world, which included David. I had no idea this was part of it. Had Pauline experienced a separation away from Snowy? I wondered, as I waited to hear from David. Why hasn't he called? Was Alice all right? I didn't know he had tried to call. At the same time, I was in pain and trying to cope.

Later David told me how much this worried him. He felt powerless. I felt like a shivering rabbit caught under a barbed wire fence not knowing how to get away. Apparently, I really shocked my body when I became a vegetarian so quickly, coupled with me stopping drugs without the supervision of a qualified doctor. I was in major detox! I learned a lot about this process as a result (Unfortunately, the hard way.)

Ludshott was a haven of peace. In the garden I was surrounded by multiple evergreens whose scent filled the morning dew as I walked amongst them. Many mornings I sat alone in my room watching the raindrops on the window in the silence. I had regular shiatsu treatments with Michael Skipwith, who has become a close and trusted friend. Some of the pieces of the puzzle were beginning to link together as he guided me in how to meditate. Each morning I would go to the small chapel and listen to that small voice which was starting to awaken. My inner sunlight was returning.

During those treatments, my heart opened, freeing me from the tensions I had collected. Michael referred me to many sacred teachings, especially Ramana Maharishi, who was an influence in his life. He had spent many months in Ramana's ashram (spiritual retreat) and knew its quiet truth. Ramana's main premise was for us to ask, Who am I? It emphasised that there was a place beyond all thoughts of such Beauty, but was covered with veils of illusion.

Once one touches that place, all beliefs of what is important change. Your values and priorities change, influencing and inspiring your choices. You no longer need to seek to be kind, caring and loving because you discover that is what you truly are. Instead of being a human "doing," you become a human "being." Who AM I? reveals that kindness and compassion is the true nature of us all.

David was away on tour. So once my health was restored, Michael took me to a lecture of Sir George Trevelyan, founder of the Wrekin Trust. Sir George is considered the Father and Herald of the New Age of which many were aware from the sixties. He quite resembled the actor Peter O'Toole.

There he stood: tall, grey hair, chatting with someone. He had an aura of such purity and majesty of heart. Michael knew him well and introduced me. Sir George embraced me. I lost my linear awareness within that embrace. I moved out of my body into the universe. Literally, I saw myself travelling through the stars. Where was I? Just in that moment, he shook me out of it. He knew where I had gone and I didn't have my seat belt fastened, nor did I know how to land.

We were to meet again many years later at the home of the Baroness Di Pauli in St John's Wood. It was a gathering of great philosophical minds, wise elders. During tea, I found the moment when I could relate the story to him. With a glint in his eye, Sir George said to me, "I so love this modern era. An elder chap is allowed to give young ladies a hug and a kiss on the cheek without it being an offence." He was in his late 70s.

When I returned home from Ludshott, Dr. Sharma put me on a vegan diet with lots of remedies. I was inspired to take yoga lessons and meditate. David was super. I remember how he tried to meditate with me, but it didn't last long. He even stopped eating meat at home. But the troubles with the band were still growing. David started to grow more silent and I am sure my change along a more spiritual line added to his pressure. We were so young and caught in many rounds of growing tensions. He tried to honour all the changes on the practical level because of my health. Something stirred, like a little pinprick in his side festering.

No tomatoes and no peanut butter was part of doctor's orders. Tomatoes are part of the deadly nightshade family and I could only eat them if they were homegrown with no pesticides. Peanut butter is not a nut but a legume and it clogs the system if eaten in quantity. I had to be especially careful. No more peanuts and beer at the pub. I didn't even take aspirin or have any drinks with caffeine, only herbal teas. Not even Coca-Cola with my pizza. "Pizza? Coca-Cola? Peanut butter? Cheese? What is that?" was the question for years from friends. Then there was the hurdle of asking for a glass of sparkling water at a party. That was a more difficult one for everyone to accept, though it is much easier now. Looking back, one could say Dr. Sharma was a forerunner of eating organic and so was I. In a land of meat and potatoes, and aluminium pans, it was not easy then.

Meditating was a jewel. It helped me to breathe through any pain that life challenged me with, from headaches to indigestion. It helped me to stay in contact with the breath of life instead of the shortness of panic breathing. Luckily, a few years later Dr. Sharma said that it was time for me to start eating 10% rubbish foods and return to eating vegetarian since I ran the risk of getting too precious. Too precious for a rock 'n' roll existence especially, as there was limited access to the foods I needed away from home, while on tour, or on holiday in foreign countries.

David seemed ok with it all, for he would eat what I cooked at home. Many have made humorous comments that he would eat meat when I wasn't looking. And Emo said that he would secretly go to the pub for a steak and chips. I only noticed this when we went to a restaurant. I didn't require him not to eat meat. I was a great cook. And as time went by, people didn't even notice the difference. It was a difficult period for vegetarians in those days, not to mention for a vegan. Eating out became more a social affair for me, a gathering of people I loved. I was healthier and that was all that mattered.

Most people, including David, had little understanding of its virtues. Even David's parents, Doug, a geneticist, and Sylvia, a film editor, both from Cambridge, came to me upset one day. They said that I was going to kill their son and their granddaughter, Alice. We had ongoing discussions. I give them credit, for they did their research and eventually adopted a very similar way of eating. Time passed and I became more knowledgeable about food combining and a more balanced way of living. Sadly, it did start to weigh upon our relationship.

At first, I think I was so excited and full of beans that perhaps I was rather too much to handle for others who still were into drugs and hard living. I felt I had found the elixir of life and wanted to share. I wanted to tell the world, which Americans tend to do when inspired. The British and Europeans are different, and life kept showing me how to 'walk the talk in their world.' I was learning how silent proof of harmony, peace and joy really sells the story. But at the time in England, being inspired along a spiritual path, including being vegetarian or vegan, was rather challenging for most, except for The Beatles, who we were to get to know many years later.

TIME OUT TO FLY
DAVID GILMOUR RELEASES SOLO ALBUM
1977-1978

Something snapped in Montreal. The strain of the lifestyle accumulated over ten exhausting years was sucking the heart and soul out of the band. Over the years Pink Floyd's audiences had changed from an attentive, devoted mega-cult hanging on every last resonating echo to an awesome, often unmanageable mob that responded mostly to spectacle. They were drunk and high beyond being more than a crowd of lonely people. Empty faces feasting on the creative spirit of their stars, less concerned with what the lyrics were saying, less inspired by who the band really were as people. They were Pink Floyd! That was it!

Each of the band had their way of dealing with the situation. During all the stories told of what we all experienced, another one was growing within David. It seemed there was less and less motivation to create together within the band. Roger dominated. There was so much bickering and idol interest, especially after the *Animals* tour 'In the Flesh'. David wondered: had the Floyd achieved all that they wanted to achieve? Maybe there was nothing else they could do creatively? Perhaps they were spent as a band? One thing was for sure: as an artist, David needed to get out of the cage that was building. He needed to fly.

After the *Animals* tour the Floyd had a year off. During this time David was at home writing songs which eventually would become his first solo album, *David Gilmour*. There were moments when he would express his apprehension, his fears, but ultimately, he had to dare to awaken his true spirit to create. His love of being at home began to melt the tension, allowing the emotions to be set free in some of the songs. 'No Way Out of Here' drifted over the night, revealing what had laid beneath. 'When you're in you're in!'

Fortunately, David's smile returned as he sat by the telly with our first daughter, Alice, eating lunch. Those moments together in the stillness of our home remain in my heart. I still hear their laughter as he rolled over on the grass tickling her, often chasing the doves as they gathered on the drive.

The gigs were a family affair, a gathering of friends, musicians and family. David's smile was wonderful. Rocking 'n' rolling again! Time out, at least for a while, until we returned to *The Wall*. I often said, and continue to say, that 'Run Like Hell' and 'Comfortably Numb', written by David initially for his solo album, went on to save *The Wall*. It offered hope within the chaos; so needed in the face of the financial challenge that lay before us.

THE BUILDING OF THE WALL
FINANCIAL TRAGEDY
1977-1980

We were facing potential financial disaster. Norton Warburg was proving not to be the best advisor for our financial affairs. Since *Dark Side*, we had been in need of advice and had turned to Andrew Warburg. I remember David saying once that he really didn't want to go into having investments. He preferred just to bank the money and wanted to keep it simple. However, the sums got too great to keep it humble. Therefore, unlike other bands who were taken by their managers, which the Floyd had under control, their accountant took them. It seemed to sneak in under the floorboards, catching them off guard. Norton Warburg eventually crashed and Andrew left the country ASAP.

The band had to find a way out of the mess and they were unprepared. In the past, they had a rhythm of touring, recording, touring and time off for writing. They would come together and an album would be born from their collaboration. This time it was different. David, Nick and Rick had worked on solo projects previously to *Animals*. Roger was the only one with ideas on the back burner that were ready for use immediately. He had two suggestions which might be possible for album projects: *Bricks in the Wall* and *The Pros and Cons of Hitchhiking*.

They met at Roger's for days. All they did was argue. "No, that is awful. No, that one is terrible." I can't speak for the others, but David returned home grumpy. I don't blame any of them, as it was a huge problem to resolve. They were on the edge of a sinking ship worth maybe

£12,000,000, payable to the taxman. And the bank balance was low thanks to Warburg's bad investments. Finally, after much discussion and debate, they decided to work towards developing *The Wall*.

We returned to Lindos that summer. We stayed in Auntie Mary's house, the Museum, in order to oversee the conversion of our house on the other side of the village. David had been playing the demo tape over and over throughout our holiday. It was excruciating. Roger's pain was so deep. I will never forget when, one afternoon, David emerged from the sala (a Lindian living room) shaking his head saying, "I don't think I can really work with this. I have no idea how this could become something people would enjoy listening to. It is just angst!" But he had to in order to rescue us all from our financial predicament. He had no choice, we thought. So the real work would begin back in the UK in the autumn.

One of the highlights of that summer was when Simon and Garfunkel, along with Carrie Fisher and friends, arrived in Lindos bay in a HUGE cabin cruiser. Carrie and Simon were on their honeymoon. Garfunkel gifted them with a Mediterranean cruise so they headed for Lindos to visit Melissa, who was their good friend.

Dixie and Alice, otherwise called Dixie and Pixie, were waddling up the hill from the beach behind them chatting under their breath, "She doesn't look like Princess Leia!" "No, she doesn't have any buns!" Oh, out of the mouths of babes! We were all invited to hang out on the boat each day. Carrie wanted to go shopping in town so Emo volunteered to take her around. He was staying with us that summer at the Museum. As for us, Lindos was becoming his home in the summer. Rick and Linnie Wills (David's bass guitarist from Jokers Wild) were also staying with us, with their first child, Nicky. As Emo and Carrie were turning one of the corners, they all met. Nicky exclaimed, pulling on Linnie's skirt, "Oh look, Mommy. It's Princess Leia!" Someone recognised her without her buns and white dress. Emo said they all smiled and said, "See ya' later at dinner," and walked away on their shopping adventure. Carrie commented to Emo later, "I haven't been called that for a while."

So *Star Wars* had come to Lindos. We had a very grand dinner to celebrate their arrival and our growing friendship. Emo sat next to Carrie. Being a S*tar Wars* fan, Emo raved about how wonderful the movies were, and how David and I had got him premiere tickets when it first came to London. It meant so much to him to think there would be two sequels.

He said she freaked! She felt trapped. She went on to share a lot of stories of how that movie had compounded upon her life. Some good, but most troubled. Here he was, expressing his love for the movies, and instead he came face to face with the reality of the star who brought so much joy in his life. It was sad.

As I relate this story, I feel this too has been our challenge, as it is with most people launched into fame. The story plays over and over. The temptation to go down with the pressure, the adulation and the lack of your own life is great. We were sometimes drowning, trying to hold on to the Beauty and Love in our hearts. We walked hand in hand in front of the adoration, caught between the glamour and "Who am I?" Caught between the art and the lie.

TAX EXILE
SILENT BEAUTY DISAPPEARS
BEHIND THE WALL
1979

It was around March-April when David came home and said that we had to do a tax exile year. English tax laws were such that this would be the only way to get out of our mess. With our income bracket and the possible income tax liability from the Warburg affair, we had no other choice. The word exile made us tremble. The thought of not being able to return to our home without David for a year was weird. It brought an understanding and more compassion for my mother. It reminded me of the times Ron, my stepfather, had gone on isolated duty in Libya with the Coast Guard for one year. It reminded me of when he went again to Alaska for one year. The tension in the family was not something I wanted to relive. We had to go with David.

Overnight, we found ourselves packing and leaving the country ASAP. We went back to Lindos, as our house was nearly ready to live in until other plans materialised for where the Floyd would continue to record. I interviewed several ladies to be our nanny for our year away. Sue Turner entered the fold. Eventually, we would relocate to a home near Super Bear Studio in Berre-les-Alpes, France, where the creating of *The Wall* would further manifest.

In addition, we asked our dear friend Christian Mouzon to come as family support while David was working. We had grown very close during our time in Turkey and we thought he would be a perfect addition to our team. He was French and as only David spoke French, he would be a great asset to us at home. The process was swift as I recall. By the time we settled in Lindos, to my surprise, I began having not only morning sickness but also afternoon sickness. I was pregnant with our second child.

Our home in France was a lovely ground level French stone structure amongst a forest of pine trees. It was hot, but we were graced with a swimming pool to cool us down from the summer heat. Alice and I often played on our rubber rafts in the late afternoon sun splashing about like little kids. I was getting rather pregnant and often sought refuge in the shade.

Some afternoons we would have rain showers. Waiting for the rainbows, Alice and I could be found in our bikinis, lying in the garden at the back of the house in the rain, arms out. I told Alice that the rainwater in the mountains was good for our hair and our skin so we would lie there happily getting soaked. We would giggle and laugh together. Sometimes she would put her ear upon my growing tummy and speak to her next brother or sister with loving words.

Some days I would go with David to Super Bear. There were very special walks down the road from the studio. The air was always full of the scent of pine and mimosa. The branches hung down over the path laden with yellow fluffy flowers and the morning dew would wet my face as I parted them along the way. There was a moment during my first walk amongst this wonder of nature that I had such a fright. Bathed in its Beauty as I was, I parted the low-lying pine branches when unexpectedly the path abruptly stopped. There I was, teetering on the edge of a deep ravine. I felt off balance with my pregnant tummy hanging out before me. Leaning against the rock face next to me, taking a moment to stand still, I regained my composure.

To continue I had to walk carefully along a narrow path to the left. I felt like a mountain climber, minding each step for fear of falling. It was majestic. Over the years, the winds created bonsais amongst the rocks below and across the cliffs on the other side. Eventually, I found a place to sit and bathed in the silence surrounded by this breath-taking beauty.

I meditated, chanting sounds of peace and love for my baby growing within. I felt I was in a Zen temple moulded by nature, hidden away from the ordinary passer-by. When I could, I would visit my secret place where I found peace with Mother Nature. It seemed Heaven was upon Earth there and it nurtured my soul and my baby.

It was not so within the walls of the studio. The contrast between the calm of nature's temple and the creative process amongst the band made it rather difficult to be there for long. As time went by, I especially found it painful to witness Rick losing his self under the pressure of Roger's growing domination. Since *Animals*, there started to be no room for Rick to express his innate qualities, nor David, but David persevered and found a way.

Others have written that Rick had nothing to offer, but I feel there was another contributing factor that created this difficulty within Rick. There was no room for his true soul to enter, which I will explain later. What also made it difficult was the fact that he was often the punching bag. The camaraderie of the band's relationship was always boy tease boy, but for me this was getting to be too cruel. Rick buckled. It was heartbreaking to watch. Nevertheless, I feel there is another invisible aspect that turned off his creativity.

In writing this, I have discovered that Rick was inspired by Stockhausen, a German composer who's known to be "one of the great visionaries of 20th-century music" (Wikipedia). He was known for his groundbreaking work in electronic music, aleatory (controlled chance) in serial composition, and musical spatialisation. I can see his influence in a lot of Rick's compositions and playing.

But as Roger's need to have his vision dominated, his inner turmoil increased. It did not make fertile ground for such music to grow, or for David's intuitive way to bring forth that silent flavour, the flavour which both contributed to within the sound of Pink Floyd. Upon reflection and some research, I was unearthing an invisible aspect of this time, which I had never considered, buried under the Wall.

From an energetic and spiritual understanding, the force of such deep angst (ONLY I AM, THIS IS MINE) closed the doorway to the Beauty they had created in the past. Consequently, it was quite a task to create harmony, a struggle to transform such negative emotions. It was often said that Roger was determined to get his way, often in sacrifice to the music. Out of desperation, the band became involved with transforming Roger's shadow instead. It was an uphill struggle. Things had to change and did eventually. However, it did leave its mark on all of us.

Many Floyd books reference Roger this and Roger that. They all seem to talk about him being the visionary and yes, he did carry those elements. In his banter, the world forgot that the Floyd were a creative gestalt, within which were many aspects needed to have made their music happen. Some are visible, some invisible. All that we have read built the image that Roger was the main force keeping the band going forth. The stories do not acknowledge another level of vision, which transformed Roger's melodrama into something of archetypical Beauty. It came through the work of the whole of the group. The suffering turned to hope hovering in the darkness.

Somewhere I read about Roger's excitement—about how the audience would be able to experience the show from all angles, sound wise, as he stood high up in the auditorium. 'Sound in the round' was one of their wonderful qualities. This special aspect always touched me. It so brought the audience into a union with the music. I am taken back to Ann Arbor when I first heard them playing. Great sound travelled around in the space where we sat together while they were creating magic.

In fact, not many groups then even had a good sound balance. I would ask David, "Why were there not more groups using it? Why don't they have good sound mixing? Surely, they must realise that we want to hear what is on the albums!" It was always one of my niggling comments after many concerts that we went to throughout the years. I definitely had high standards, I suppose thanks to the Floyd's vision.

I discovered more about the visionary Karlheinz Stockhausen, who was one of modern music's most controversial figures. His commitment to technological innovation, particularly in electro-acoustic musical techniques, has ensured a legacy of lasting influence. Stockhausen understood his musical ambitions as an attempt to restore music to the position of philosophical and ethical significance it held in the ancient world. Recalling the ancient Greek conception of music, he remarked that "the highest calling of mankind can only be to become a musician in the profoundest sense; to conceive and shape the world musically." He argued that human imagination and sensibility was increasingly dominated by the visual field, and that we were in danger of forgetting how to use our ears to ground and orientate our awareness of the world. He considered his work as a composer in terms of an attempt to 're-attune' mankind to its environment.

"In 1958 Stockhausen called for new kinds of concert halls to be built, 'suited to the requirements of spatial music.' His idea was a spherical space which is fitted all around with loudspeakers. In the middle of this spherical space, a sound-permeable, transparent platform would be suspended for the listeners. They could hear music composed for such standardised spaces coming from above, from below and from all points of the compass. His music dealt with the integration of all concrete and abstract (synthetic) sound possibilities (also all noises), and the controlled projection of sound in space giving the impression of movement in space. Towards the end of his creative life he finally achieved isomorphism of the four parameters of pitch, duration, dynamics, and timbre."

https://www.deutschegrammophon.com/en/composers/karlheinz-stockhausen/biography

As I read this, I thought: goodness, that sounds familiar. Perhaps intuitively this too was the driving and inspirational force which made the essence of Pink Floyd pre-*Animals* and *The Wall*. Did they know? I never heard it discussed and if they did, it was behind closed doors or perhaps before my time. But honestly, it probably would have gone over my head then.

What spoke to me was between the lines in the silent spaces of their music. It continued to be over the years. Time and time again, it elevated their audience and me beyond ordinary existence in those concerts and albums. It certainly touched my paradisiacal heart. Repeatedly we fell into the timeless euphoric blending within the drama of the lyrics. The silent message of Beauty beyond the conflict, offering a way to transform the challenges of the treadmill we have created. Did they know?

There is no need to have any understanding of any theory. For me, it does not need any explanation. Beauty just is. It has the power to unite. What David and Rick brought to the table started to be compromised more with *Animals* and then *The Wall*. It had become our life, the conflict. It was in our tissues, in the air that we breathed. We were to become like the frog who, when put into cold water and the heat is turned up, slowly dies. We didn't jump out.

As we went deeper and deeper into the birth of those albums, we all succumbed little by little into being those albums. I do not think Roger's viewpoint, quoted in many books, is truly the only explanation of the creative process for those two albums. He felt David wasn't interested, Rick had nothing to offer and Nick was just a good friend and more interested in his cars. He was the drummer. Quite often, he expresses that he worked through the Floyd banter because he wanted to help the others through the difficulty. I think there is another side to *The Wall* not mentioned. It was really our soul struggle to "BE what we were born to BE." To clear the way so we could live the highest potential and shine!

For sure we did work through difficulties together, the band, Bob Ezrin, James Guthrie, Steve O'Rourke, and the families, as we went deeper and deeper into the transformation of Roger's troubles and his visions. So often, the pressure in the room could be cut with a knife. So often, there were days our hearts silently wished not to have *The Wall*.

I watched David's quiet and sometimes not-so-quiet influences bring music to us that spoke of hope, outside the lyrics. I saw his struggle. He tried so hard. I watched Rick's withdrawal give a podium for a victim within the subconscious aspects of the story. I watched Nick's struggle between friendship and finding his voice.

Ultimately, they each served in their own way to make those albums an archetypal transformation, of what challenges we all have in life, i.e. to truly find freedom, peace and beauty. It may have been Roger's visionary story and perhaps Roger should have had the courage to face his demons alone. Maybe it was actually his trapped soul trying to get out.

Perhaps it was God speaking to us. Perhaps it was greater than all of us. Often great art is a gift for humanity. Upon reflection it was certainly evident, but we turned away. Roger and Caroline hid in their own limo, chose a different hotel and a different caravan while the torment continued. Realisation was waiting but didn't come. Perhaps the process was all of ours, which is why we are still not released. The struggle, the conflict, the pain, the beauty, all became our lives, even now. We, too, became the gestalt hitting against the wall and blindfolded. Sometimes the disciple is the last to know.

Rick left the band on paper, and in secret agreed to do the gigs. Unable to confront the ever-rising tide, Rick disappeared into history after *The*

Wall tour. However, his essence remains on those albums that went before. The drifting silent beauty of his melodies carried on in other ways with other outlets. He wrote *Broken China* dedicated to his third wife Millie and collaborated with Dave Harris on the album *Identity*. In 1994, he was officially reinstated into the New Pink Floyd so the sound began to fly again. His last performance was 6th September 2007, the premiere of David's concert 'Remember That Night' at the Odeon Leicester Square, London.

In September of 2008, at the age of 65, Rick died at home of an undisclosed form of cancer, leaving an unfinished solo album, supposedly comprising of a series of instrumental pieces. Did the music of his soul come just before his spirit called? I wonder? David was moved and published a tribute to Richard Wright on 15th September 2008.

"No one can replace Richard Wright. He was my musical partner and my friend. In the welter of arguments about who or what was Pink Floyd, Rick's enormous input was frequently forgotten. He was gentle, unassuming, and private, but his soulful voice and playing were vital, magical components of our most recognised Pink Floyd sound. I have never played with anyone quite like him. The blend of his and my voices and our musical telepathy reached their first major flowering in 1971 on *Echoes*. In my view, all the greatest PF moments are the ones where he is in full flow. After all, without 'Us and Them' and 'The Great Gig in the Sky', both of which he wrote, what would *The Dark Side of the Moon* have been? Without his quiet touch, the album *Wish You Were Here* would not quite have worked. In our middle years, for many reasons, he lost his way for a while; but in the early Nineties, with *The Division Bell*, his vitality, spark and humour returned to him, and then the audience reaction to his appearances on my tour in 2006 was hugely uplifting and it's a mark of his modesty that those standing ovations came as a huge surprise to him (though not to the rest of us). Like Rick, I don't find it easy to express my feelings in words, but I loved him and will miss him enormously."

MIRACLES DO HAPPEN
OUR BABY AND ME SAVED
1978

While in France, I was in my sixth month of pregnancy. I was lying on our raft in the pool and there were many wasps flying about for that time of the year. When they do, they tend to hang out near water to get a drink. In this case, it was our pool. I went into the water for a dip and when getting back onto the raft, I was stung. (Not once, but twice.) Within the hour, I went into an allergic reaction and I took to my bed with severe pain in my right kidney.

When David came home, he took charge. He called Dr. Sharma in London for advice. He said, "First you must bring in the paramedics and then let me know what they say." France is very sympathetic to homeopathy but my condition had accelerated beyond having a remedy. Two paramedics wearing dark blue entered our bedroom and examined me. They said to David that he should get me to the hospital quick. That I should have my kidney and my baby removed, otherwise I would not survive.

I had never experienced such pain in my life. I held on to the bars of our headboard each time the spasms came. I cried, I screamed, I hoped Alice would not hear. David called Dr. Sharma back and gave him the report. He said, "Get her on a plane tomorrow. Give her one shot of Champagne and one shot of brandy every hour until she gets on the plane." I did not drink in those days so I got a bit tipsy. It did the trick so that I could make the journey back to the UK by myself.

David drove me to the airport and took me as close to my gate as possible. He had such concern on his brow and I could feel his heart was aching. He had to stay and needed Sue and Christian. I was not worried because Dr. Sharma was to meet me at the airport when I landed and I could feel my angels. He took me to his clinic on Seymour Place in London, which had two adjoining houses. One was the clinic and the other was his home. At the top of the clinic was a spare room reached by a connecting door, which became my home for a few weeks.

He put me on a drip of a special mixture and other remedies. I have no idea what really happened since I was numb with pain, delirious. At the end of the week, he told me that I was off the critical list. I would be able to keep my kidney and my baby, but I would have to take care for a long time even after the birth. By the end of the second week, he said I could leave and be with David and Alice. They had gone to Lindos, while the recording was in the process of moving to LA.

Dr. Sharma gave me the ok to go to LA with David on the understanding that I stayed in my bedroom most of the days. LA did not have the best air for me to heal or live in under these circumstances, especially as I was pregnant. He let me go under one condition: I had to have an air conditioner, ion machine and air filter.

An additional surprise gift to us was that Dr. Sharma said he didn't want payment for his time. He thanked me for putting such trust in him, because he had learned so much through the experience. He only wanted us to pay for the medicines and the medical tests. David and I left smiling as we set off on our next adventure to Los Angeles and the birth of our second child.

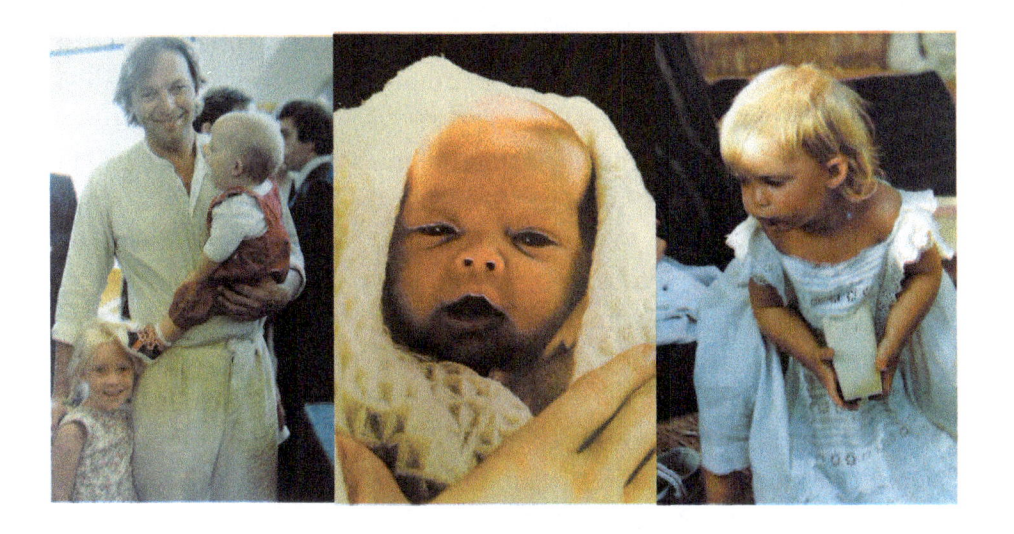

ANOTHER CHILD IS BORN
CLARE
1979

The entire band, including our manager, rented our own houses. Ours was 712 Rodeo Drive in Beverley Hills. Most of the homes we rented belonged to very rich people, some stars, some CEOs. It seemed this was the usual way to do things in LA. They were full of paintings, sculptures and precious furniture. We had a maid named Louella and community gardeners. Louella looked like Aunt Jemima from the movies of the twenties and had a heart of gold. She became invaluable to our daily life, especially her smile.

Life began to fall into place after a few weeks. David went to the studio, I stayed in my mountain air retreat upstairs and we enrolled Alice in the local Montessori school. Sue and Christian were still with us and would drive her there and pick her up. The children would be playing on the playground when they arrived each day at midday. Alice's face lit up, happy to see them as she ran across the playground. She was so cute with her blonde ponytails flipping in the air. The heart of our home was growing each day.

We fell in love with the Wholefoods shop. It was heaven for a vegetarian like me, so much choice. They would spray all the fruit and vegetables with water each night to keep them fresh. There were so many sprouts to choose from that I had never known existed: alfalfa sprouts, buckwheat sprouts, fenugreek sprouts, mung bean sprouts and the list went on and on.

The band had quite a schedule and problems were stirring in regard to Rick. A decision came forth that he must leave the band. A deal was made, which allowed everyone to save face and complete the album that they had started. The intention was a gradual withdrawal from the unsuspecting public. In addition, part of the deal was for Rick to continue to do the gigs for a pretty sum. He agreed.

Then discussions about royalties came... this is my memory of the event. I was in my last month of pregnancy when we all had dinner at a Japanese restaurant. David was in a mood when I arrived, with everyone's tensions riding high. Roger wanted to remove 'Comfortably Numb' from the album. It was one of the only songs which David had a major credit for and he *exploded*. I think if he had known karate the table would have split in two! I will never forget the look of shock on everyone's face, especially Roger's. I have only seen David lose his temper once and I hoped never to do so again. In the end, 'Comfortably Numb' stayed, and to this day, it is considered one of the best songs on the album.

I have said it before and I shall continue to say how hard I find it to understand the way royalties work. Having watched the transformation of Roger's angst into something that the *Animals* and *The Wall* albums have become, David and the others deserve more acknowledgement. And these are not just the words of a devoted wife. 'Comfortably Numb' symbolically represented the release of all the tensions built in that album. Without it, we certainly would have gone down under the weight of the stone. Needless to say, David and Rick's intuitiveness as musicians influenced the whole album.

David soared to the heights of Beauty when he let go, playing 'Comfortably Numb' with the rays of white light behind him. That moment proclaimed from the top of the wall sending us hope! I know that many lead guitarists feel that it is the best song on the album. I have to agree. Every time I was at the mixer at the gigs of *The Wall*, it was 'Comfortably Numb' that took my breath away and uplifted my heart. It was a relief, a testimony that we can be free from the stone.

I finally found a midwife. Her name was Merina and she was gentle and angelic. I particularly liked the fact that she was still breastfeeding her child of three years when we first met. I was happy, for she was a true spiritual midwife. We met regularly and practised our breathing exercises, sharing our mutual vision. We made a great team, ready for the day our child would enter the world.

David and I waited and waited for that moment to come as I was ten days past my expected due date. The Floyd kept working and working to finish the album. On the evening of 1st November 1979, David returned home and said the album was finished. No sooner did he say that than I went into labour. It was clockwork. The gates were open and she was born in the wee hours of 2nd November 1979, full of light.

To this day, I know the baby waited for her dad to be there (and the album finished). It wasn't a long labour. It was a girl. We named her Clare for a radiant glow that surrounded her. David went and fetched Alice into the room to greet her new sister. Together, David and Alice took baby Clare into the candlelit bathroom and had a bath together. In addition, Alice took with her a life-size doll we had given her as a present. I think it was a bit crowded.

While they took care of Clare, Merina finished dealing with the placenta, later buried under a new lavender coloured rose bush in the garden. We were all tired, especially David, but joy overcame us as we held our wee Clare in our arms. Within hours, flowers, cards and telegrams surrounded us and the phone didn't stop ringing. The house filled with the sweet scent of hundreds of flowers.

Little by little, our life integrated another child to care for, while the Floyd had a breather preparing for the next cycle, the gigs. We rented a large camper van and we gave Sue some time off. Kids in tow and Christian by our side, we set off up the coast of California, destination Big Sur, in a large American camper van. As I chose to breastfeed, it made it easier to travel with a young baby. We met up with Crosby of Crosby, Stills & Nash, who lived up that way. We walked on the beach of Big Sur at sunset. Alice followed her dad, walking in his shadow, and I took pictures of the moment with Clare carried close to me in our baby sling.

When we returned to Los Angeles, I was tired, so we hired a vegetarian cook named Akasha. She made the best corn bread and azuki bean stew with Hijiki seaweed. I learned a lot from her as we explored the world of vegetarianism together. Clare started to cry a lot, especially after midnight. David and I took turns walking around with her. During the day, Louella was a great help for she was a real MOM-MA. She had had nine children of her own and she would walk around the house with Clare in one arm and dust with the other. It gave me time off to rest.

Her screaming became rather disconcerting. Maybe there was something wrong. Eventually, I found a homeopath and an alternative doctor who helped me with a way of eating as an experiment. He hoped we would discover what was bothering Clare as I was still breastfeeding her. We started with me stopping dairy products for one week and then introducing one thing for a few days and seeing her reaction. Then I would go on to excluding wheat. The first try proved that it was dairy, but it was not her having difficulty. My kidneys were not digesting dairy well and it was going into the breast milk. She was fine after I stopped eating dairy.

I personally feel that as we had had that near death experience during my sixth month of pregnancy, she too was behind in the development of her organs. This would come to light later when she was around two, for she could not tolerate milk. She is fine now, she says. Later, back in the UK, Dr. Sharma suggested that we should put her on to soya milk, which was organic in those days. GMO was not in our vocabulary then. We were just not aware of it.

As David's schedule was very demanding, I took on the total responsibility of breastfeeding Clare without him giving her a supplement bottle as he had done with Alice. This meant that Clare came everywhere with us. She was a wee one going to all the Hollywood parties. I was in a back bedroom feeding her once when Andy Warhol walked into the room. We sat on the bed chatting for some time and became friends. He said for me to call him when we got to NYC and we could go shopping together. I particularly wanted to see his studio.

THE WALL COMES ALIVE
LOS ANGELES
1980

The months of December, January and February involved creating the next step of Roger's dream. *The Wall* was to become a multi-media theatrical production. Some have referred to it as a 'dramatisation of angst.' Really it was a 'dramatisation of how to transform angst' for me. Rehearsals began and day after day, over and over, the Wall came down. On one occasion during rehearsal, I said to David, "Wouldn't it be nice to have a positive ending amongst the rubble?" The next time I saw the run through, all the band were stepping out over the rubble playing acoustic guitars or other simple instruments. Lovely.

The Wall gig consisted of only two venues in the States, Los Angeles (seven shows) and New York (five shows). The idea of taking it on the road just wasn't a possibility anymore. Thus, the way the band toured changed. All of the shows were full of everyone we knew and didn't know, from ticket holders to Hollywood stars, from record companies to musicians. David's parents came over from England to be with us and hold their new grandchild. It was a family affair. Lots to organise regarding concert tickets, backstage passes, cars to the airport, cars to gig, babysitters, restaurants, who sat next to who but the most challenging of all, for me, was the night the grand-nephew of Kalu Rinpoche (a Buddhist Lama) came.

I had taken refuge with him several times while he was in Los Angeles. In the Buddhist tradition, the purpose of taking refuge is to awaken from confusion and associate oneself with wakefulness. Taking refuge is a matter of commitment and acceptance and, at the same time, of openness and freedom. By taking the refuge (vow), we commit ourselves to freedom.

Yogi John, a dear friend, had suggested that I should offer Lama passes to come. "Do you think he would really like to come?" I asked. He was sure that he would like to come, for he had had a private conversation with Lama the previous day. The Lama was only in his mid-thirties and interested in other aspects that influenced the hearts and minds of the young. Despite that, I was still quite surprised when he said yes. I wondered to myself, "What does a Tibetan Lama need, in regards of care from me, in order to witness the Floyd concert The Wall?"

We picked him up within the appropriate time. I escorted him to the mixing desk. I had arranged seats for us, thinking that he might prefer to be in the centre of it all. The mixing area was like the helm of the starship Enterprise. The one mixing desk had expanded to two: sound and lighting. Now, the Wall was beyond description except by a technician and there are books about it. There were sections of command modules for each aspect of the production, which took up LOTS of seats in the middle of the hall. Production managers and plenty of assistants lined the desks wearing headphones, their fingers poised to begin the show. Bottles of Evian water were everywhere.

Lama walked through the audience in a cloud of unending peace, observing, feeling. The peace was contagious and entered my being softly. I felt like I did as a child always trying to do my best for my parents. I was overexcited, honoured and at the same time fearful that I might trip, catching my high heels on my long chiffon dress right before him. At the beginning, I offered Lama some earplugs. He shook his head, "No, it is ok, I will be fine." Then the music began.

The surrogate band in masks, made in the likeness of the band, first led us into a euphoric state as brick upon brick built the Wall. The Wall represented symbolically the alienation Roger had been feeling on the *Animals* tour and within his life and the band. As the last brick was put into position, his voice echoed throughout the hall, a farewell. Many words kept screaming over our heads, song after song. God, it was loud! Painful!

I looked over to Lama to see if he was ok. The stillness of his focus maintained within his being. Words of desperation called out to us from the Wall as the drama unfolded, searching to be heard. The Wall was complete. We were isolated from being one together, the band and the audience. No longer unified within the music. This time we were just alone in another's projected anxiety. Anguish of a person's pain hung in the air.

Spellbound and overtaken by the grandeur or perhaps the incredible majesty of the production, the audience was still. Numbed, held by the drama of the journey of self-indulgence into the shadow, into the pain of existence. We succumbed to the imagery and the sound of the round and the theatre of it all. The drama still plays in my head. Just the sheer volume pierced every cell of my being. It was quite a feat. Where were we going? Were we being dragged down by it all? Was this our reality as well? Were we blinded by the glamour of it all and yet held in such Beauty? What was it? Held in the crossfire? Numb?

Finally, the moment of release arrived. The lights dimmed. Stillness filled the air. David appeared on top of the Wall. His playing came from his heart. It reached beyond, piercing the fog. In that song, we transcended the angst and brought Beauty even though the lyrics led us to believe otherwise.

The audience held in rapture as the notes took us higher and higher and higher, releasing the tension. David, silhouetted by rays of light behind, moved with the sounds as his playing pierced the air from above. Waking us up from the spell of destruction, nurturing, freeing us, taking us to our resurrection. Transcending the angst within us all. No wonder Roger didn't want the song on the album. Maybe he was not ready to transcend his own pain. Yet maybe he listened to his soul telling him this was the way?

The fervour increased as Roger screamed out to the audience, asking us to enjoy ourselves. Did you really mean that? He was so sarcastic. The pace increased. Sounds of primeval screeching, drumbeats, repeating, took everyone further. They stood and danced, hypnotically clapping to the beat. Surprisingly, Lama stood with them, his poise captured in the coloured lights. And when it finished, he honoured them and clapped too, but it was silent. I understood that evening the term 'one hand clapping' for there was another energy that emanated from his gesture. It was a deep appreciation from his heart that brought tranquillity to us all within the frenzy. It was a creative force lifting and transforming the vibration already there.

I motioned for us to leave during the last song just before the Wall came down, so we were not caught in the audience leaving the stadium. The imagery spat out its vile throughout the hall as we walked down the aisles of the seated audience towards the backstage. Their heads were focused on what was happening on stage, but as Lama passed they turned. One row after another turned and saw him.

I will never forget the expressions that lit up their faces in contrast to what they were witnessing. It was as though they saw Christ. Their hearts opened with the thought that he had graced them by being there. Rock 'n' roll concerts were up until then a place where we were free to rebel, to hide out. A secret place just to be, to contemplate, to express, we thought, but Lama came. He entered their sanctuary and made it acceptable. He honoured us all that evening with his silent presence of compassion. The madness stood still for a while.

While we watched from the side lines, shouts of destruction resounded around the hall, over and over. The Wall collapsed against explosive sound effects and smoke. It was over. My head rang from all the screaming in the last few songs and from being so close to the explosion where we stood. Was it the end of the world? And there from the rubble came all the musicians playing the final song with acoustic guitars, mandolin, clarinet, and accordion. The calm after the storm.

NEW YORK, NEW YORK
FEBRUARY
1980

Next stop, New York, New York. The flight from Los Angeles was full of celebrities. Juliette Wright secured the seat next to Rudolf Nureyev. Joan Collins, with her large sunglasses, sat in the row behind us. Dudley Moore was sitting in David's seat when we were boarding. We had a moment of laughter as David said to Dudley, in a Dudley voice, "Dudley, I think you are sitting in my seat?" Dudley looked up from behind his newspaper and in a Dudley voice said with a smile across his face, "Really? OOOH, sorry David." It was a real English moment.

On one of David's free evenings from rehearsals, we visited Auntie Mary, from Lindos. She was staying in their New York family apartment and organised a wonderful dinner in her favourite New York restaurant. Andy Warhol was one of her guests; we sat next to each other and I felt at home chatting with him. The feeling of friendship that we had felt in Hollywood was still there. I had Clare with me, carrying her in a Moses basket, and had to breastfeed her during our evening. Andy was very open to discuss the nature of breastfeeding. Looking over to Clare suckling he asked me how it felt. I said that it was wonderful and created a special bond between baby and mother. I added that I wished this could be true for the dads.

He sat still in thought, when he came up with the idea that we should make a plastic brassiere, which could hold milk with nipples. The idea would be so that the dads could wear it and feed the baby. One of the bonuses would be that the milk would stay warm at body temperature. He paused for a moment, and then added, "Darling, it must be pink, of course! What should we name it?" I was not good at naming these sorts of things so I shrugged my shoulders, putting my focus back on Clare. He then said with the glee of insight, "I have GOT IT! We shall call it PINK FLOOD!" We so laughed at that one. How great… pink flood! During the evening, he asked David if he would let me go shopping with him. We shared a love of art nouveau. Cheeky, Andy said, "Don't worry, David, I will only take her to the best antique shops! Hee Hee." I reassured David that I would just buy little things. In the end, Andy and I never had the opportunity for our adventure.

We did meet up in the helicopter going to the gig on the night that we gifted him tickets. Clare came with me in her Moses basket and surprisingly slept through the sound of the chopper. The gig was outside NYC in Nassau Coliseum. It was initially booked for two dates, 25–26 February, but there was such a demand that two more dates became necessary. We took the helicopter from the New York City heliport. It was my first ride in a helicopter and it was exciting! I was so grateful that we did not have to sit in rush hour traffic to get there. We just hovered over it.

Things were different backstage. There was a sushi bar! Travelling with the band was becoming more civilised. No more dried cheese sandwiches and potato chips. Even the road crews enjoyed a fabulous spread. There was a time when they all took alcoholic beverages out to their stations. Now they took Evian water. At the last shows, I spent more time backstage with our little Clare because the volume and the subject matter were getting to me. It had been an amazing journey in many ways, but I was tired. I needed to get home. Lyrics repeated in my head as 'Wish You Were Here' was playing and penetrated through the walls of the dressing room.

I was beginning to know "Heaven from hell, blue skies from pain," and this was my life. This was all of our lives. 'Wish You Were Here!' Our marriage began during the *Wish You Were Here* recordings. Now it had become truly our journey. Sitting backstage on the large couch breastfeeding Clare, I asked myself, Where will this journey lead? Or are we "two lost souls swimming in a fish bowl year after year?"

THE CLASH OF THE TITANS
THE MOVIE - THE WALL

The Floyd had moved on to making the *Wall* movie with Alan Parker. Well, really, it was Roger, Gerald Scarfe and Alan Parker in the end. The stories that filtered back were like the clash of the Titans. David did not agree with the whole way things were developing during the making of the album. Little by little, he saw a democratic relationship in the band change to 'You are working for me. I am your leader.' There was no space for anyone to contribute under those conditions. It was really a Roger project and David withdrew from having much to do with the film; until one day, Steve O'Rourke called and pleaded if he would be a referee.

I really don't remember much of what went on because I had become pregnant again with our third child. I had to focus on my health, as my kidneys were weak from what happened during Clare's pregnancy. We were still settling in the new house and something about it was unsettling. I did worry about the house becoming our home for I felt uneasy.

Normally, an energetic sparkle appeared shortly after redecorating. It wasn't the case at Hook End. The sparkle never came, even by the time we had our open house party. How could I say to David that there was no sparkle, we have to move? He probably would think I was mad.

David would often return from a day filming with photos of the war scenes. These images often triggered memories of Vietnam for me. Roger revealed his father's story and this reminded me of the only war story in my life. My stepfather was a medic in the Coast Guard and was on isolated duty during 'Nam. He was away for a year. We could not avoid hearing stories on the news about what was going on over there. We watched the anti-war demonstrations and the world's disapproval, while we, one of the soldiers' families, suffered and worried at home, suspended in the emotional dilemma.

On April 4th, a year before his assassination, Martin Luther King spoke about the war at the Riverside church in New York. King stated:

"Surely this madness must cease. We must stop now. I speak as a child of God and brother to the suffering poor of Vietnam. I speak for those whose land is being laid waste, whose homes are being destroyed, whose culture is being subverted. I speak for the poor of America who are paying the double price of smashed hopes at home and death and corruption in Vietnam. I speak as a citizen of the world, for the world as it stands aghast at the path we have taken. I speak as an American to the leaders of my own nation. The great initiative in this war is ours. The initiative to stop it must be ours."

But the war went on and on. Demonstrations and protests continued. One thousand women marched on the White House. Students were arrested for being conscientious objectors. Students for a Democratic Society demonstrated in Chicago and I watched in disbelief as the police, on national television, hit the cameraman who was filming them beating the students. I watched. I saw it happening! And I just couldn't believe that there was nothing about it in the news the next day.

While at a White House luncheon, singer Eartha Kitt spoke out against the war and its effects on the youth, exclaiming to her fellow guests:

"You send the best of this country off to be shot and maimed. They rebel in the street. They will take pot... and they will get high. They don't want to go to school because they're going to be snatched off from their mothers to be shot in Vietnam."

But the war went on. No one was listening in power. My mother prayed each evening for his safe return. She waited each day for a letter, which did not tell us much except we knew he was alive. He kept the truth away from us. He had to as a soldier in combat. He was a Chief Petty Officer, a leader of men. The only way for us to keep our sanity was to stay away from listening to the news about the war. It is only now I realise how he often must have walked on land in the aftermath, caring for the dying and the afflicted.

Seeing the images now I wonder how he dealt with the atrocities he witnessed, especially in the night, when he got home. Agent Orange did not discriminate. It not only destroyed the underbrush, but maimed children, mothers and the elderly. It destroyed their homes, all the people in the way. In addition, pregnant women gave birth to deformed children. I still don't get why we were there. How does one live with those images? I cried today as I looked at them. Ron was there. He breathed the air. He was a witness to the devastation of a people, of his men.

Over the years after he returned, Ron would often have lung problems. My mother kept on at him to stop smoking cigarettes, but he didn't. On 19th May 2002, he passed over, diagnosed with lung cancer. It was not until afterwards, when my sister, Donna, was helping my mother with the financial closure, that we discovered something which made us weep. Apparently, he died, luckily they said, just a year before the government's allowance for families of servicemen dying from Agent Orange could claim compensation. What? Oh my God! He really died from Agent Orange. It was too late to question his treatment. It was his time to pass over. But families are still in a process with the government to get more help. Tragically, they are being ignored.

And so, it is today. The war goes on amongst men. Why do we not value the preciousness of life? The love of power seems to be more in favour than the power of love. As an artist and as a human being, I constantly seek to question the ripples I create with my images, or forms, or even with my actions or my voice. As much as I tried to understand Roger's vision of the Wall and as much as I can see how art sometimes must shock to awaken the sleeping dinosaurs it is not my way, for I know we become what we contemplate. I choose Divine Beauty. I choose Love.

ISN'T SHE LOVELY
WALL CONCERTS
EARL'S COURT 1981

The Wall concerts at Earl's Court were about to begin. The month was June and I was pregnant, not far away from the day our next baby would be with us. The countryside was a bit warm and muggy, the air rather close, so I stayed in the coolness of our home drinking homemade iced tea. David was rehearsing during the day and sometimes into the night.

One evening, 'Happy Birthday' by Stevie Wonder was playing on the radio as I prepared dinner. That song always gets me dancing. It is such a happy song. I never knew that Stevie had written it as part of his campaign to have Martin Luther King Jr.'s birthday become a national holiday. In fact, he was one of the main organisers and decided to create this single to make the cause known. The holiday, he proposed, would facilitate the realisation of Dr. King's dreams of "integration, love and unity for all of God's children." An interview with Stevie took place that evening on the news.

He was in the UK to promote his new album, *Hotter than July*, on which was 'Happy Birthday'. It was a great interview. He has such heart, joy and a sense of humour. The interviewer asked him, "Stevie, how does it feel being blind?" He responded, "I don't mind so much being blind. I probably would mind if I were black!" Then he laughed. The facetious twist held our laughter in thought. 'Wonder' what he really meant?

There were six concerts. I was rather big, so I didn't go to all of them. Furthermore, the atmosphere amongst the band had reached an all-time high, to such a degree that we each had separate Portacabins (modular buildings) backstage. To compound the dividing wall of separation, Roger and Rick had theirs turned away from the centre of the hospitality circle. Long gone were the days we shared dressing rooms together, greeting friends and family. Unbeknownst to the waiting people, it would be the last time the Floyd would play together again for nearly twenty-five years. It would be at Live 8.

The centre of the hospitality area was carpeted, and had tables with white garden umbrellas and flowers, as though we were backstage at Ascot without the women wearing hats. Many people were congregating around one of the tables. I wandered over to see who was sitting there. It was Stevie Wonder. He came to the gig and was a magnet for everyone.

Somehow, someone offered me a chair to sit down next to him. Maybe it was because I was rather pregnant and needed to sit down. Many were envious, as we chatted for quite a while. Can you guess the subject? Babies. He put his hand on my tummy, bending closer, and quietly sang 'Isn't She Lovely' for a few bars. My tummy tingled. Did he know it was a girl? We didn't. Now every time I hear that song I remember the night Stevie Wonder blessed my baby. Isn't she lovely? Yes, she is our Sara.

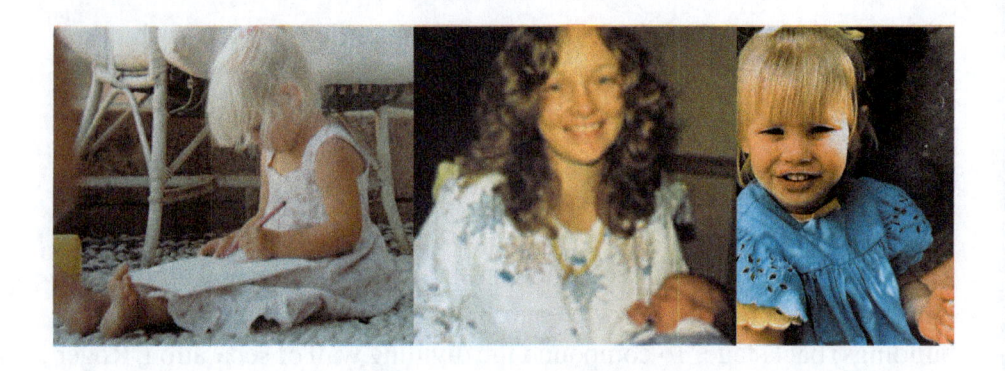

SARA IS BORN AT HOME
BROCKHURST MANSION
JUNE 1981

Then there were three. During most of my pregnancy, as I mentioned previously, I had to be careful with everything. While one is creating a baby, one's kidneys go through changes and need close attention. Mine especially. Consequently, I was tired most evenings. David hung out with Mick Ralphs when he was not involved with the filming.

By my third pregnancy, I was more and more inspired by how important it was to create an environment of peace. I wanted to allow quiet to penetrate my baby in the womb. I had a little room at the back of our suite where I would meditate each day. Again I had nausea. I remember always having a bowl of fennel seeds and cardamom on our bedside table to ease any indigestion in the night. It was in many ways an easy pregnancy. I loved being pregnant. I always felt at one with Life with a baby inside.

I had found another local midwife named Melony. We shared many hours together in the last few months ensuring we were on the same page. She seemed totally at one with my vision of natural childbirth. It was on midsummer's night eve that our third baby called, for it was time to enter the world. It was just around 8.30pm on 20th June when we had another girl, whom we named Sara. I remember the time because there was a programme I wanted to watch about Krishnamurti. I was interested in his teachings and had read many of his books.

I watched the programme as the golden sun set with me having contractions. When I close my eyes, I still feel its rays filling the room through our leaded light windows. This delivery was very different from the previous two. It was faster. As I recall, I could not stand anyone touching me except on my feet. I am sure David was at a loss after his helpfulness with gently rubbing baby powder on my tummy before. It was such a surprise, especially for me. It was so fast and intense that all I could do was to breathe and stay focused.

There was no time to educate anyone on how to approach me. Even I was at a loss. It was so intense. There was no space to speak except do my breathing and go with the birthing of our child. I just wanted to say, "Melony, please, you are so kindhearted, but don't touch me," as she continued to stroke my forehead. Somehow, I don't think it would have come out that way. Therefore, I just grinned and bore the irritation. Her and David's feelings were more important to me.

Actually, it did go smoothly and we had a perfect little baby girl. The rays of the setting sun filled the room with golden light along with the smiles in our hearts. David was wonderful as always with our wee ones. He was and is a natural born father. I adored watching them together, their hearts uniting in love. In those moments, we were so happy. The birth of a new soul to one's care is wonderful. Unfortunately, the afterbirth pains weren't so wonderful. With each subsequent pregnancy, they got stronger and stronger as the womb sought to contract. They were awful! When it came time to put her to the breast they intensified. I knew that was part of the purpose, to contract the womb, but it was painful. The delivery contractions seemed far easier in comparison.

Family life went on. I remember the early mornings in the kitchen, next to the Aga, preparing the kids' breakfast and packed lunches. The house had not awakened yet. I would be up very early with the sunrise, listening to the early morning chorus of the birds with Sara. I would feed her and then sit her in her little reclining bouncer on the floor next to me, warmed by the heat of the Aga. These were special times together in the stillness of the dawn.

I would prepare the school lunch boxes. I made wholewheat bread sandwiches with cream cheese, cut into shapes of words. LOVE was my favourite. The L was topped with a carrot, thinly sliced. The O was a slice of cucumber. The V might have been nori-seaweed, but I have forgotten.

The E was more of a challenge to cut any vegetable. I had to make little pieces. Each day I would spell a different word. Their lunch box would have fruit and cartons of apple juice.

So there we were, Sara and I, each morning, with me being creative by the dim light of the kitchen. Everything was an opportunity to be creative. Sometimes Sara was so quiet that I almost forgot she was there. She would just sigh and giggle. She had and still has a very placid and deep meditative nature, which I treasure. All our girls were blonde beauties with pigtails and bows, still beautiful as their blonde locks have darkened. Their tender hearts remain precious to me despite the challenges that make them cry or make them angry.

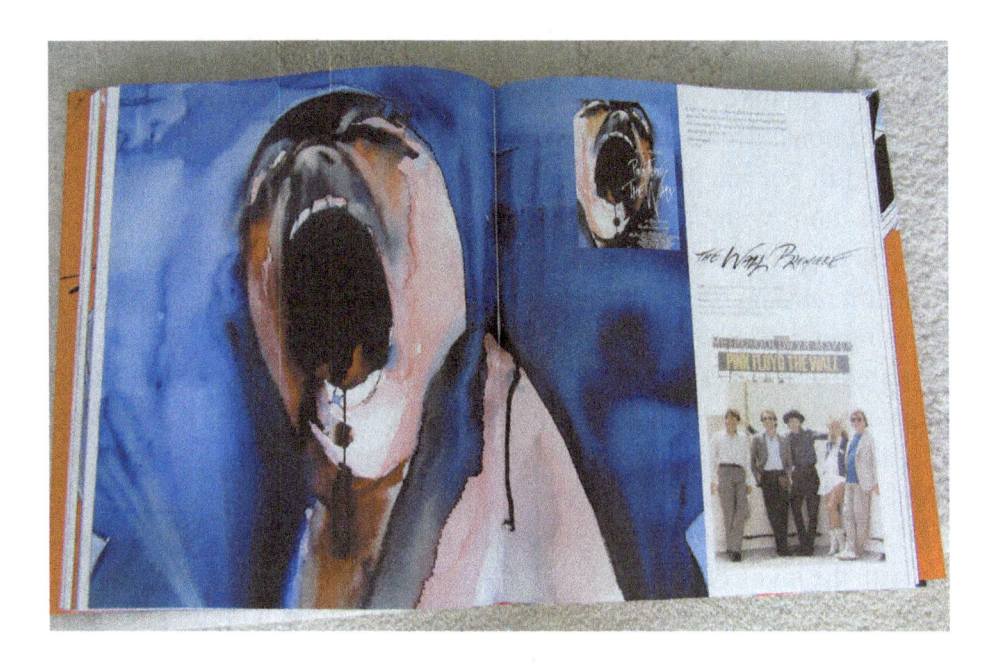

"WHAT WAS THAT?"
THE WALL PREMIERES
1982

Finally, the film was finished. We all travelled to Cannes and hung out on the beach during the day, watching all the people pass by, waiting for the moment to see the show. *The Wall* was one of the last films shown in the old Palais; it had seen better days. The Floyd had upgraded the sound system and it was so loud that the paint literally fell off the walls. It fell like fine snow onto our heads, leaving a distinct impression of dandruff on us all.

Alan Parker, the film director, is quoted as saying, "I remember seeing Terry Semel there, who at the time was head of Warner Brothers, sitting next to Steven Spielberg. They were only five rows ahead of me and I'm sure I saw Steven Spielberg mouthing to him at the end when the lights came up, 'What the f***was that?'"

David and I spent a lot of time together with Bob Geldof and Paula Yates while we were in Cannes. I so admired their dry sense of humour, full of intelligence about world affairs and philosophy. They were so sharp with their wit and at the same time very down to earth. You couldn't pull the wool over their eyes. We had such a lark cruising the after show parties. When we returned to the UK, Bob and I had regular phone conversations. I remember sitting in our telly room at Hook End Manor slumped in our navy blue comfy chair, feet over the arm, having long conversations with him on the phone.

I had hoped to find a couple of dresses for the premiere in NYC. Olivia Harrison introduced me to Liz Emmanuel, dress designer for Lady Di's wedding dress. She then took me further into the fantasy when she appeared with a dress that Carmen Miranda would have worn. The shape was very flamenco-ish with a kick skirt on the bottom. It was scarlet with a fuchsia lining which appeared as I walked. I loved it! I was set. Two fabulous dresses for the premieres.

Unfortunately, I went into shock a few days later when Liz presented me with the invoice. It was over £5000. I had to let go of Carmen Miranda. Barry Lyndon was much more affordable. The dress had already been custom-tailored for the film. It fit me and was on sale. Carmen was a new creation needing adjusting. At the time, and still, I am not used to having a designer of her fame make a dress for me. Nor could I justify spending so much on a dress for a few evenings, no matter how beautiful! I had to turn it down before she started to work on it. I was rather embarrassed, but she totally understood. I think that one of my daughters still has the Barry Lyndon.

Wonderful dresses became important to me because over the years I found it difficult to deal with all the women who fancied David. Women always projected their goddess onto him while at the same time they would project psyche daggers of jealousy at the woman in the way—in other words, me. In the process, they would analyse me first to see what they were up against, then judge what their chances were and how to destroy the love connection— hoping David's eyes would shift to them. Fortunately, David seemed oblivious to them. But I knew the energetic game women on the hunt play. I was sensitive and very aware of the feminine wiles. It was shocking to me at first, being a small town girl. However, eventually I discovered a way to insulate our relationship and myself.

I started to empower my own beauty with divine dresses. I put myself high up amongst the stars in the heavens, beyond reach. I loved the period of Fred Astaire and Ginger Rogers. They were my role models. As a young girl, I used to dance in front of the telly, dreaming of the day when I would dance with Fred Astaire. I so wanted to be one of the dancers in a Busby Berkeley production as well, but I knew that time had passed as it was the 80s.

My vision regarding the groupies was an easy task to achieve. London was full of amazing antique dresses of the twenties and my collection grew. And it was affordable! I was still sylphlike and they worked perfectly. One day I found what I felt was simply the best, at the Antiquarius Antique Market on the King's Road, Chelsea. It was such a find.

It was a dress that made me feel like Cinderella, somehow; I felt safe within its gentleness. I loved this dress so much. I could almost sleep in it. It was to the floor, in a delicate fabric, pale pink with appliqué blue lace flowers. The cut flowed like a tulip in the wind. I would always put a Ginger touch on my outfits, bringing them into the twenty-first century rock 'n' roll look. In this case, I wore a mini blue jean jacket and platforms, which allowed me to tower above the groupies and yet be elegant.

It was to become a challenge, later, holding up the image as my inner journey began to call me to ask the question, Who am I? It was one thing to create a wall of protection and yet another when it began to separate me from David and even myself. What I meant is that we hid from the truth of the pain and consequently closed our hearts from each other. As time went on all of us were taken deeper and deeper into the story of the making of the Wall.

Our own walls were being built, which not only isolated the band from each other, but also within our personal lives. It was as though grey smoke had covered our ability to discern darkness from light. Sometimes I just wish I wasn't drowning in it at the time. Perhaps things might have been different? A friend once said to me, "Ginger, when those thoughts arise, take life as it is—then make it special." That wisdom has helped me so much to accept the twists and turns in life and create Beauty as the journey still goes on. I wish I had known that at the time. The emptiness was so difficult.

SEARCHING FOR HUMILITY
SOHO LONDON
1983

As time passed, my path was leading me more into conscious awareness of my humanity. A little glimmer of light was entering my heart despite the world of Pink Floyd. I was becoming aware that the ripples that I created either separated me from the world, or joined me together in community spirit with everyone upon the Earth. It was important to feel the gentle breeze of my thoughts as I walked down the street sending a smile to passers-by. A smile, not in need of acceptance, but from a desire to give because everyone seemed so beautiful. Life was hugging me each day and I wanted to share it.

Sir Paul McCartney and Linda were creating a film based on his love of the Rupert the Bear stories of his childhood. It was a short film, *Rupert and The Frog Song*, which had its first release in 1983. Sir Paul sought to capture the sense of wonder and adventure in childhood that never dies within us all. Perhaps it awakened a memory forgotten? The innocence of the animation and the music certainly captured my heart, especially the theme song called 'The Frog Song' also known as 'We All Stand Together'. In 1986 it became a hit and the animated film received Best Music Video at the Grammys. To this day, the joy in the film has often found myself and my children holding hands singing, along with the frogs on the telly, dancing and rejoicing together. Now it is our granddaughter's turn. Thank you Sir Paul and Linda.

While Paul and Linda were in the final stages of its completion, they asked David to play on the song during the final credits. The video was released in 1984 and we were invited to attend the premiere held in Soho. I decided that I wanted to dress low-key and work on my humility in the public arena. The quality of humility was coming more into focus on my Journey and path of return to God. Could I handle not being noticed, standing out in the crowd, standing by my famous rock star husband, humble?

So, I wore a long gabardine white skirt, white boots with a white jumper with tiny, embroidered flowers knitted for me by Rita, who cared for our house. The premiere was held in a club that seemed very dark inside. Everyone was wearing black, which was the fashion at the time. I was astonished as I walked to our seats, for my plan did not work. I stood out like a light bulb, as I was the only one wearing white. I was extremely noticeable as the spotlights panned over the crowd of famous and not-so-famous people. The story went on into the next morning. Johnny Walker on his morning radio show spoke of the evening and the lady in white. I would have to try harder to be less conspicuous, if that was my wish.

CECIL COLLINS CLASSES
ILEA, LONDON
1983

Days went on. The children went to school. Dinners were shared with friends. I started to paint in the little room off our bedroom. Before long, I began art classes with Cecil Collins. When I entered the classroom on my first day with Cecil, I felt as if it was a homecoming. After attending a few classes, Cecil asked me to bring in a few samples of my artwork. There was one particular painting which held his attention.

It was a watercolour of a winged being, crouched in a foetus position. The figure sat upon the water's edge below a Greek-like mountainous scene. It was one of a being, broken and waiting in contemplation, forlorn. Cecil, peering straight into my eyes from behind his glasses, said with such clear compassion, "The next time she flies, her wings shall not be made of wax." I decided to call this watercolour 'My Icarus.'

Further into the term, Cecil said that he did not want me to do any artwork for two years except to come to his classes. So I did this as per his request. It proved interesting to wait and allow something new to grow within me. These classes were like the apprenticeship of old, working under the tutorship of a master, in many ways. As it came to pass, I continued to come to his classes one afternoon a week for nearly eight years. I am so grateful to have experienced so many formative and inspiring moments with him and the other students. It tingles and fills me with a smile as I remember them.

One afternoon I came to the class with my abundant American spirit and smile. Cecil was sitting there just by the door in his tweed suit, yellow wool waistcoat and tie. His arms hung loosely across his chest. He sat there with his usual meditative look from behind his tortoiseshell glasses, waiting patiently as we all went to our desks. Just as I came into the room, he ducked. With a Cecil chuckle laced with wisdom he said rather directly, "Ginger, you shall have a real smile on your face one day!"

Boy! He put me through my paces from then on! Usually, no matter what instruments, tones, pace, or positions he put us through, my drawings were always perfect, something petite and cute. Then one day he worked us hard. He had us moving with the model, and then quickly—drawing faster—faster. My head was in a swirl! I had to let go! I struggled to hang on but there it was ONE BIG FAT BLOB of black yuk! A new beginning.

I loved his wisdom. I loved how he touched us within our classes, awakening our innate creativity. Later it would come to pass that I would meet Elizabeth Collins, Cecil's wife, who was said to be his muse, his inspiration. In fact, they say that Cecil painted Elizabeth. So Elizabeth was the woman behind the man.

In one of his BBC documentaries, sitting in the corner of the pub, he commented, "One day I discovered, as I listened to the songbird from my window in the early morn that the song and the bird and me were one." Further along in the documentary there was a shot of Elizabeth and Cecil walking together. I felt their union. They were the songbird, the song and were one. This experience has become mine too. Each morning from my window I am one with the robin and our song.

I forget how long it was before Elizabeth asked if I could come for tea. I felt so honoured to have their private telephone number so we could arrange a time. The day arrived and I set out for Paulton Square, just off the Old Kings Rd in Chelsea. I knew where it was for my favourite boutique was on the corner. I asked the taxi to drop me off on the corner and slowly walked down the street to their house. I rang the buzzer and was let in. They lived upstairs and the hallway was narrow. It was quiet, almost too quiet as I was nervous but excited. As I entered, I wondered silently to myself: What am I to experience? It isn't rock 'n' roll but I like it.

Behind The Wall

Kathleen Raine lived on the first floor. She was a poet, a philosopher, a critic and a scholar who wrote mainly about William Blake (the renowned British artist of the 17th-18th century), W.B Yeats (poet) and Thomas Taylor (English translator and neoplatonist who was the first to translate into English the complete works of Aristotle and Plato). The Collinses and Kathleen used to be close friends but had a falling out. Therefore, there at the top of the stairs was a white door separating them from each other.

As I climbed the steep stairs, my attention was held as I passed from one William Blake print to the next. I was very fond of his work and his philosophy. Elizabeth opened the door to greet me. She was tall, sylph-like and a rather beautiful elder woman. Her hair was greying, with an up-do, Gibson style. She had Parkinson's and her body was frail but her blue eyes shone as bright as the sun reflecting upon a pool of water.

Their living room was on the top floor, another two flights to go. Cecil's artwork covered every wall. There were little canvases and larger canvases, many of which I was familiar with from his book. Sadly, the narrow space and the amount of paintings hung so close to each other made it difficult to take in the sheer delight of the moment. Nor could I as I was following Elizabeth and needed to stay focused.

On the first floor, we passed a room filled with canvases and papers piled high in the corners. Paintbrushes of many sizes in containers and paints were everywhere. The energy of creativity and poised inner silence oozed out from the door. I could feel the timelessness that would engulf me had I entered. I assumed that it was Cecil's studio. He was not home that day. I passed the doorway like a ship in the night, graced, allowed to witness part of their life.

We entered their living room where the sunlight cast its beams of light onto the colourful pillows and carpet. Elizabeth motioned for me to sit at their small table while she made us tea in their little French maisonette kitchen just outside the door. That day began a special friendship. Over time, she would share many stories about the evolution of their relationship, which gave me insight into mine.

Cecil often told us of how, in his early life, he had a sword that he often used upon his paradisiacal heart. Then one day he awoke and saw its true purpose was to protect his paradisiacal heart, not to destroy it. While speaking to Elizabeth and listening to her stories, I learned her part. She said, "Ginger, I came to realise that there was a bigger story we were participating in, for humanity. From that day onwards, I sought to do my part creating the vision that Cecil and I were given to do. As a result, all the little conflicts between our personalities disappeared. We both woke up and dedicated each other to it from then on. That is when our relationship changed."

It was a special afternoon, the sunshine, the cakes, the tea and Elizabeth. On one of the walls, Cecil had drawn in his unique way a caricature of her. He called her Bell. Mrs. Tweedie was right when she said that Cecil painted Elizabeth. Sadly, it was time to depart, for I had been there for hours. It was time to descend down the stairs back into my daily life. My mind and soul tingled from being with her.

I was inspired to walk more along the path she walked with Cecil in their marriage. It was wonderful, and yet, could we—that is— David and I? As I was leaving, she stood at the top of the stairs silhouetted by the light and called out to me, "Ginger." I stopped and turned around to listen. She said, "Don't forget your Angels!" The truth of her voice held me for a moment. I smiled, turned and left with my heart uplifted. Her final statement was to guide me silently within, as its seed grew over the years.

CECIL EXHIBITION
ALDEBURGH, SUFFOLK
JUNE 1984

Cecil was exhibiting in the Festival Gallery in Aldeburgh, Suffolk. Many of his students were going so I got a ride. He was exhibiting 44 paintings and I so wanted to see them in the flesh. During class, he often spoke of the Journey to the Lost Paradise. That within each individual, there is this secret place, often untouched, under-nourished. He sought through his art to unlock the door, to feed and sustain the viewer. He wanted us to dwell within its mystery, within its poetic symbolism and intention. He wanted to catch the soul in its return to Paradise.

His journey had not been easy, but his vision held fast. Within the intellectual and artistic communities, he found he was alone except for Elizabeth. He challenged the conservatism of traditional religion for he drew Christ's resurrection full of light and freedom. He challenged the iron clad 'art for art's sake' with his symbolic images and expressions of the spirit within us, which they denied its existence. On that day, I stood within the grace of his struggle and the Beauty he attained for us all.

I was especially moved by the painting called 'The Hymn of the Night.' Cecil approached and said with a wry tone in his voice, "This painting always seems to make people pause and some even raise their umbrellas to it!" I asked "Why?" for the images didn't seem offensive. He chuckled in his Cecil way, which always seemed to put me at rest. He continued telling me in a whisper of confidence, "I think it had more to do with the Anima." It was to do with acknowledging the feminine within our hearts. I stayed longer, pondering his words. And as I did so, I felt a mysterious chill about the painting.

Before me was a young girl standing in front of a bountiful tree, arms crossed between her breasts, eyes glowing, beckoning one to enter. The full moon captured the time of our entry, guided further by an angel, while swans floated below the mountains in the distance. Was this mysterious chill drawing me into the "woman" in myself? Was I ready to look? Could I dare to go further to reveal what lies deep within? Was my Animus aligned to support this process? I saw and was inspired by the power of art to challenge the viewer through symbolism and intent to the journey of return and holism.

These questions did not evoke a desire to raise my umbrella and spit at the painting. What it did do was place the experience deep into my subconscious memory of the day that someone would raise an umbrella at my work. And they did. My work also created tears of joy. It has helped me to remember that this was a good response and not to get discouraged.

This witnessing of his work was a very important exhibition for I awoke that day with a strong desire to be open and create artwork which uplifted and sometimes even stirred the viewer to question. Cecil gave me a tool to weather the storm and create the light within in just a few words, the colours, the images and his chuckle. I bless him every day for daring to follow his soul purpose to serve God through his art and his life. I am grateful he chose to be our teacher and make his wisdom accessible for us all, whether rich or poor.

GUY FAWKES
BROCKHURST
1984

Every November, we had a bonfire party with fireworks. At the time, I never quite understood why, on 5th November, England celebrated the burning of the effigy of Guy Fawkes until years later thanks to Wikipedia. Its history begins with the events of 5th November 1605, when Guy Fawkes, a member of the Gunpowder Plot, was arrested while guarding explosives the plotters had placed beneath the House of Lords. Celebrating the fact that King James I had survived the attempt on his life, people lit bonfires around London, and months later the introduction of the Observance of 5th November Act enforced an annual public day of thanksgiving for the plot's failure.

Within a few decades Gunpowder Treason Day, as it was known, became the predominant English state commemoration, but as it carried strong religious overtones, it also became a focus for anti- Catholic sentiment. Puritans delivered sermons regarding the perceived dangers of popery, while during increasingly raucous celebrations common folk burnt effigies of popular hate-figures, such as the pope. Towards the end of the 18th century reports appear of children begging for money with effigies of Guy Fawkes and 5th November gradually became known as Guy Fawkes Day.

Fortunately, all this had changed by the time I landed in the UK. I also think very few understand the symbolism behind their firework parties. (Around the late 90s, I decided to discontinue having them for I think Guy

Fawkes had paid his dues.)

Nineteen eighty-four was a special year for Michael Kamen, a dear friend and composer. He asked if we could make a recording for the latest Monty Python movie, *Brazil*, with everyone singing in the studio. There were always many friends and children invited so it was a perfect setting for his request. I remember our girls at the edge of the stage in swirly skirts and sneakers, hand in hand bopping to the music of the band throughout the night. Nick Laird- Clowes and his band the Dream Academy played because David was producing their album. Their song 'Life in a Northern Town', released later in 1985, still fills my heart with nostalgia as I often listen to it. It was a crisp evening, and the lyrics caught the flavour of England and the night.

George Harrison and Olivia plus their son Dhani came. They had become close friends and lived in a nearby village, Henley-upon-Thames. We stood by the fire warmly wrapped. Slipping into the joy of the evening, we watched David absorbed with the fireworks. David had been on duty creating the firework display with helpers throughout the day. He loved setting off the fireworks each year. We organised bales of hay in the field next to the fire for people to sit on with marshmallows on sticks waiting to be toasted.

Kegs of beer sat on the edge of the field next to the coal-fired barbeque, which Rita and Jack tended. The smell of hamburgers, sausages and cooked onions filled the air between the smoke of the fire and sulphur. This was one of David's favourite times of the year. I could see he was full of joy when the fire light touched his face each time he passed to set off the next firework. There were lots of 'Ohh's and 'Ahh's.

It was near the end of the evening when we all gathered again in the studio where Michael instructed us on what we were to sing. David and a technician were in the studio ready to record from behind the glass window divide. Mikes were set. The room was full, with everyone in good spirits. The recording began. It wasn't until 1985 that the movie *Brazil* came out in the cinemas. Terry Gilliam, one of the Monty Pythons, called it part of a "trilogy of imagination" and a testimony to George Orwell's *Nineteen Eighty-Four*. It was a satire about the craziness of our awkwardly ordered society and the desire to escape it through whatever means possible. It was not successful at the time, but it's now considered a cult film.

Monty Python has become part of being English. They were our generation of cultural satirists. Many waited each week—we certainly did—to watch their television series *Monty Python's Flying Circus* and looked forward to the release of their films. I still have them all on DVD. Eric Idle became a dear friend and we often had sushi together when we were in London.

When I first arrived in the UK David took me to one. It was like watching a film in another language without subtitles. The humour combined with the accent was beyond me at first. I just sat there in the cinema breathing in all the smoke from the audience's cigarettes. Years later, the silly walk and curry's brain would become part of my vernacular amongst many more like nit, nit. I get it now. And the song at the end of *Brazil* always reminds me of that firework party at Hook End many years ago.

FLYING AGAIN
ABOUT FACE
1984

After the recording of *The Final Cut*, it seemed like there was a final cut in the relationships within the band. Rick had already left, not amicably, during *The Wall*. Roger had turned further to dominate, trying to exclude David from collaborating with the concept for *The Final Cut*. The theme primarily focused on a critique of the Falklands War as well as Roger's personal betrayal from his father again.

The Floyd needed to produce another album to comply with their record contract. Roger's vision and his one pointed drive after *The Wall* pushed him on. He thought the Floyd was his. Consequently, this did not leave much creative room for David to participate. Nor inspire David, for Roger's energy was like a little boy clinging selfishly to his toy ('It's mine, it's mine'). Besides, what for? Why should David contribute? The original way of creating an album was gone. In fact, how could he under those circumstances?

During this cycle, I felt that Roger should have gone it alone in his own creative process, but the ties that bind still held on. Besides, the record company wanted a Pink Floyd album, not a Roger Waters solo album. Did he use the lads when he should have had the courage to let go? He insisted he was doing them a favour. With strings? Who can say upon reflection? Tensions ran high. Nick is quoted as saying, "If we do nothing maybe it will go away." Neither David nor Nick were not having fun. Nor did they feel it was over, despite Roger treating them as though they were not there at times.

The album certainly was not the Floyd we knew and loved. Nor was it reflective of group metamorphosis. The delicate sounds of Rick's piano and David's distinct voice were almost gone. Roger's angst once again appeared without the balance of the others. But David held on. The Floyd was part of him. After so many years, 23 to be exact, Roger could not just say, "It's over!"

I supported this in whatever way David deemed necessary to maintain his honour. Bob Geldof said during the filming of *The Wall*, "Democracy on the set is a hundred people doing what I tell them!" That statement was true on the film set. It was about Roger and Alan Parker then, but the truth of the comment also applied while recording *The Final Cut*. It was apropos for Roger, who was freezing David and Nick out. It was far from a democracy as he worked on the basis that the writers should have the final say!

I stayed away from the studio most of the time. Family life was full at Hook End. In fact, I don't think I have ever listened to the album. I had had enough of the sound of war and conflict as the sound of Beauty was disappearing behind the wall that still stood. I could feel the winds of change and prayed for a fruitful one.

David spent a lot of time over at Mick Ralphs', formerly of Mott the Hoople and Bad Company. It was boys together smoking and drinking, playing guitar and laughing for a change, having fun. He had decided to take some time to reflect and do a solo album, as at the time there weren't any future plans for the next step for the Floyd. Over time, it began to manifest and Pete Townsend helped with its birth as a co-writer. Bob Ezrin, Michael Kamen, Andy Jackson and James Guthrie came on board once again.

This meant that there was some semblance, some continuity of what went before, but with more space, more freedom for David to create. It was an opportunity to step out of the part he had been forced to play with the Floyd in the last few years. He wanted to dare to open up again creatively, which did not mean he was giving in to Roger's belief that it was over. He just needed to fly, to breathe again. It was a very joyful phase. His team were so supportive, not only creatively but also in heart.

David said in an interview from the *Source*, "Doing this album I wanted to make a really good record. I did not want to do it very, very quickly, and I wanted to get the best musicians in the world that I could get hold of to play with me. So I thought I'd just make a little list of all my favourite musicians, you know, best drummer, best bass player, best keyboard player, and I'll work through the list to see who I can get. Jeff Porcaro was top of my drummers list, Pino Palladino was top of my bass players list, and Ian Kewley, or the Rev, as he is known, he actually came and did the bulk of the Hammond and piano playing and he was terrific. Steve Winwood was top of my keyboard playing list but he couldn't do most of the album, but I got him to do a bit. He played Hammond organ on 'Blue Light.' I had a bit more time and was feeling a bit freer about things on this album... just more 'accidents' tend to occur."

At the same time, it did feel like we were walking on eggshells. Roger had announced that he was leaving the band and for sure, he felt the band was finished! We were in shock as the story began to unfold. David was caught between self-preservation, being driven by his determination and right to go forth. Plus, he was wondering if he could do it alone. Was he too stuck in the formula? Was the formula actually his way forward? Time would tell.

Right now, he had to focus on *About Face*. Questions floated between the creative lines of his thoughts: what will my listeners think? Can I play to smaller audiences, in smaller halls, without a huge production? Who am I? Many of these thoughts were kept silent, or came and went as he focused on the birth of *About Face*. Some he shared. Some he did not.

ABOUT FACE TOUR
1984

The time was approaching for David to form a band and take *About Face* out on the road. With the album set to release in the UK on 5th March and in the States on his birthday, 6th March, David was almost certain of who was going to join him. The general line up, with other guest appearances at individual concerts, was: Gregg Dechart (keyboards), Mickey Feat (bass guitar), Jody Linscott (percussion), Mick Ralphs (guitar, vocals), Chris Slade (drums), Raphael Ravenscroft (saxophone, flute, keyboards). I went along for the first few gigs in Ireland.

The first show was in Dublin. When we first arrived, we all went to our rooms for a rest and a shower before going to the hall for a sound check. Mick Ralphs was in the middle of taking a shower when a rather impatient knock came at his door. A man from the hotel was shouting in a strong Irish accent as he continued to pound on the door, "Mister Ralphs, Mister Ralphs?" Mick shouted back from the bathroom, "I am in the shower. What do you want?" "Well, Mister Ralphs I have ah' telegram for ya." Mick shouts as he gets out the shower, "Can you slip it under the door!" "OHHH, NO! Mister Ralphs! I cannot be doin' dat' for it's on a tray!" Mick's eyebrows raised in disbelief as he wrapped himself in his bathrobe to answer the door. It was one of those unbelievable moments that marked the story of our journey to Ireland.

The next stop would be Belfast. We had to walk through the checkpoint barricades to get to the hotel. Ever since I had arrived in the UK, this situation of North and South Ireland was always in the public conscience.

There had been incidents of IRA bombings or killings every year since I arrived in 1971. However, I was never so close to being in the energy of confrontation between groups of people as I was that day. The smell of possible bombing loomed in my mind throughout our stay. At every corner, I tensed, wondering, is this the moment? The fear of the reality was so alive in me.

Despite being an American and raised with the day-to-day tensions of the four fears: IRS, cancer, communism, and nuclear war, I still could not get my head around this situation. The indoctrination did not prepare me for the possible reality. Any moment there could be an explosion. Any moment a person or many could be dead. Their anger and desperation appeared suspended in the air, saturating the walls, hanging on the faces of the people.

Many years later, I was to return with the healer and mentor, Lily Cornford, as her assistant, treating patients. In fact, we saw at least twenty people per day. I was training with her in the art of Mental Colour Therapy. It is a form of healing based on the healing power of colour and love. I saw another side of the Irish during that week. Lily was so well received, especially when she spoke about the angels and the wee folk, the elves and the fairies. The crowd lit up at her lecture each time she spoke of them. It was special to be in a culture that believed that they existed without a doubt. In the evening, they would share stories of their folklore and times when definitely they met with an angel or two. It was different from the fear of war.

After Ireland, David went on tour in Europe, where they all travelled in one of those big buses from gig to gig. One part of him, as a musician, needed to be out there sharing his music. He loved the buzz and the interaction. The other wanted to be at home. A great composer once said, "You can write the greatest piece of music, but if it is not performed before the people it doesn't exist." This is so true. Performing was and is so very important to the creative process. Just as exhibitions of my art and creativity are essential to me. One is given the ability to create in order to serve and uplift others. We are co-creators of the world we live.

After a while of living out of a suitcase, David began to miss his morning cups of tea and the girls playing around the kitchen table with the dogs. He missed his wife and the warmth of his home. It warmed my heart to hear him saying that in his video of *About Face* for I deeply missed him too. I was so happy because he was happier. But I missed him terribly.

At the end of the month, they were to perform in London at the Hammersmith Odeon. We were so overjoyed that he was home again. His lyrics about being home again captured the truth in his heart. I loved watching the girls jumping into his lap in the morning as he watched telly and read the morning newspaper, their blonde pigtails catching his face as he tickled them. In fact, our dogs were happy to see him as well.

The London gig was a happy affair. It was an affair of heart with family, friends, and other musicians, most of all when Nick Mason and Rick Wright joined David on stage and played 'Comfortably Numb'! What I remember the most was how joyfully David moved about, playing with such exuberance, smiling. Mick was a great partner for him as they inspired each other to the next riff. They laughed together as the sounds reflected their mood. It was a pleasure to witness their friendship through the music as they played. This album and tour would prove to David and the world what a great musician, songwriter and producer he really was when free.

My favourite song was and still is 'Out of the Blue'. I remember how touched I was when David first played it to me. To this day, I feel that it's a message from God for us all. It is a message that did come from out of the blue. It holds an archetypal message within its sorrow and pain. It was as though David spoke from the love deep in his heart as a father and as a man. It is an inner testimony of how he really felt within the shadows of his being. He spoke for all the children, for all the parents, for all of humanity.

> *"Out of the blue on the wings of a dove*
> *A messenger comes, with the beating of drums"*
> 'Blue Light' on album *About Face*

Next stop was Canada, then on to the USA. We would meet when they reached the Big Apple and played at the Beacon Theatre. We decided to take the girls, Alice, Clare and Sara, and Annie Rowland, our nanny. My brother Stephen was to meet us at the theatre. I hadn't seen him in years and suddenly my little brother was no longer little. He was tall, with the heart of a teddy bear, plus a huge beard and long hair. Goodness. He took me aside at one point and said "Charlie, Mom just told me that your father was not my father." With a lump in his throat he asked, "Charlie, Why?

Why, after all these years did she wait until now to tell me?" Charlie was the name my mother continued to call me.

I was rather taken aback at the news. It appears that after leaving my father she met the love of her life. (She thought) she was a fragile soul, alone in the world after leaving Daddy. She always had been alone. Her mother, my grandmother, was the youngest of twenty-two children in Boston. During the war, food was short and the girls sold their hearts for extras. My grandmother then went on to have four children, which she eventually put into a Catholic orphanage. She was a prostitute.

My mother was four years old and her stories of that time were rather bleak. She had to scrub the floors, even at four—no time to be held, no time to be a young child. If she wet her bed, the next night the nuns would put her bed with her in it out on the balcony in the freezing winter. As the snow fell, she shivered with panic and fear of freezing. Their intention was to stop the problem. Did it? I wonder.

She didn't get out of the orphanage until she was twelve. There were several tries to have someone adopt her, but all failed. Her life became the life of an orphan scrubbing the floors and going to mass and being whipped on the head if she fell asleep. Where was the Christ spirit then? She has passed over now. Just before, she said that she was grateful for the nuns because they did give her Christ; therefore, she forgave their trespasses. She had travelled far to reach that point of insight and true Christian love. She had lost her way for a while. She felt guilty about her divorce and having a child out of wedlock. She hated Christianity for a time but had returned to it. She could finally find peace.

I pondered what Stephen had just told me, as we stood outside the Beacon in the afternoon sunlight. I thought, well, at least Stephen was born from love. Over the years, more would be revealed about this affair. I partly understood my mother's dilemma for in those days it was not acceptable to have a child outside of wedlock, so she made up the story that my dad was Stephen's dad.

Sadly, and consequently, for me, the lie made each phone call and vacation with Daddy a problem in regard to ever mentioning Stephen. The years of covering Stephen's hurt as he pleaded to speak to his dad came flooding back. I was young but the eldest. He would tug on my sleeve, "Charlie, Charlie, I want to talk to Daddy!" My heart went out to him once again as he shared his new heartache.

LIVE AID
WE CAN FEED THE WORLD
1984

We were staying at the Sunset Marque in Hollywood, California and I invited a dear friend, Laurie Scott, over for lunch and then to the show. It had been years since we had been together. We had so much to share; lots of children's stories to tell. We met first in the afternoon at the hotel while David was doing his sound check. She was very involved with the Ethiopian crisis. A crisis? It was the first that I had heard of it because caring for my children kept me focused in another direction. I found the information she revealed very shocking. They needed help! We presented the information to David, who was open to participating in doing a show but in the UK. I wished that I played guitar so I could do more.

Laurie only had a three-week window to organise things and discuss it further with us, as we would be going to Lindos after returning home.

The concert was to be called 'One Life, One World' and to be held at Wembley Stadium on the 9–10 of March 1985. She was pushing time but miracles do happen. Jonathan Weston and Henry Newman were her main team. We allowed Laurie the use of our London Home on Maida Ave until they secured offices.

Harvey Goldsmith was to be their promoter, thanks to our connection. She was operating on a shoestring budget and worked day and night. Her heart was so motivated to succeed in helping the starving people in Ethiopia. She was inspiring many. Germaine Greer called out to the world saying, "All they have is dirt! For God's sake, we must help them!" The fervour was building. Her cry for help still rings in my head whenever I read her words.

It was a major task and I was a novice. Laurie had worked and organised many events previously for humanity. She was a trooper. I had spoken to Bob Geldof often since the making of *The Wall*. He said that he would support it. The climate of the day with many stars was of great resistance. Many were suspicious of anything like this at the time. It was hard work inspiring them.

Even George Harrison came to David and advised him not to let me get involved. He said, "I went through a nightmare for nearly nine years with the tax man over the Bangladesh concert. In the end not many were helped, just the lawyers." He continued, "Your heart may be motivated, committed, devoted, but getting it done, then facing the process of the tax man and then making sure the money got to the people, is a nightmare. Don't do it!"

I think this cast a cloud over David. I continued, but I felt like a salmon going upstream. I had lost my ballast. Laurie and I met with Bob at Fortnum and Masons and asked if he would give us support getting acts. I created a poster, which Bob said directly, as he does, "That's too pretty." We still chatted most days on the phone, as we were friends. There were many other meetings searching for sponsorship. Time was passing and each day 40 people were dying under those white tents in the baking sun. The tide was turning but not in our direction. Both Laurie and Jonathan worked day in and day out, struggling to find the light at the end of the tunnel, hoping for a miracle.

In October 1984, images of millions of people starving to death in Ethiopia's famine were broadcast on Michael Buerk's BBC News reports. Bob saw it and was shocked. The images were riveting and went deep. It further motivated him. He had to do something to help. He called Midge Ure, hoping to get him on board. They formed Band Aid with the intention of recording a single to raise money. In December, Bob, Midge and many stars got together and recorded 'Do They Know It's Christmas?'

This started to change the momentum in the minds of many stars. In America USA for Africa recorded 'We Are The World'. Despite this, Harvey Goldsmith withdrew from our concert, which was a great disappointment. Later we were to discover why. Bob was called by God to carry forth the mission. None of us knew this at the time and it was not the way we thought. We were just carried along by the tide.

However, the suspicions did not stop there even though the record was a success. Band Aid money was still questioned, but despite this, Bob Geldof had the tenacity to badger the stars and the moneymen. He played the game and went to Ethiopia with the supplies. He wrestled with the press and succeeded. Bob was described as the "terrier that wouldn't let go." He announced to the press, "I am going to do my own f***ing concert." So that was it.

Harvey left our ship for another. Looking at the video of the making of Live Aid, I understand more the process he and Harvey went through to make it happen. I did not have that capacity. The wind in my sails could not have gone the distance as they did. I passed the gauntlet within my broken heart to them. Laurie was beyond disappointment when she heard the news. She was heartbroken almost beyond repair.

The times were a changin' in London, to add to the tension. London was all a-rage with fighting. Violence was everywhere in England. The music scene was difficult too. Everyone thought Bob was making money off the idea of a live international concert. Many thought the idea was just another way to fame, and they were going to be used. They thought the money would be misallocated into Bob's pockets instead of the starving populations; suspicion was rampant. We had the same difficulty. "HELLO? Why is it so difficult? Why not? These are starving people. Why doesn't your heart say yes?" We were little guys with heart. Bob had a mouth.

To make it worse, he was considered a foul mouthed, fading pop star in dirty clothes and unwashed hair. They shouted, "Why should we listen to him? Why should we do it? What a bizarre idea!" Most were frightened it might flop and tarnish their image. (So many egos). Were they that fragile? Nevertheless, Bob pushed and pushed and pushed. I wonder how many times he said the f*** word. George was right; it could have been a nightmare for us. We didn't swear.

There was a moment when I exploded months later. A fiery beast arose when I read in our daily papers that Bob was considering pulling out. He was considering pulling the plug. With what I know now, I do understand, but then rage took control and I learned to swear. I called him. "Bob, you took the horn away from our concert for a larger one behind my back. I cannot deny it, it was very hard not to feel hurt and ever consider speaking to you again. It was challenging to find understanding, compassion and then to support you. But if you do not do Live Aid now, it would be absolutely tragic and a sin! YOU MUST DO IT!"

As time has passed, I have come to so admire him. I have joined the flocks that call him Saint Bob—even if he resists the term. His candour makes me smile. His tenacity I admire. During that time, he became the world's champion. No longer just a rock star disappearing from view who swore on stage. No longer was he some guy in a film depicting an addict in a rock band's movie about a wall. He was a modern day hero. His soul was doing what he was born to do. Live Aid rocked the world into action, at least for a while. What a mantle he now carries. What responsibility of power does he wield?

July 13th, 1985, has gone down in history as the day that music changed the world. Curiously, but not so curiously, in the end everyone tried to get a spot in the show; the phones were ringing into the night. Bob, Midge and Harvey, including many others, were on tenterhooks until the very end. They had the acts. What about the stage? Nevertheless, they did it! The world had 16 hours of music that brought tears of joy to many. I watched from home, as I was pregnant with our fourth child. It would be too hot and the day would be too long for me. In addition, we were moving house. In the end, David went and played with Brian Ferry and returned home with many stories.

The story of Live Aid will always live on in my heart with gratefulness. It was a vast learning curve of the need to help humanity and opened my desire to serve. But it left me asking: how may I serve more? My answer to that question would come as the years passed. Honestly, I could not have come close to what the boys—Bob, Midge, Harvey and their team—achieved to create Live Aid. Therefore, I do hope somewhere, somehow, our efforts did help to make it so.

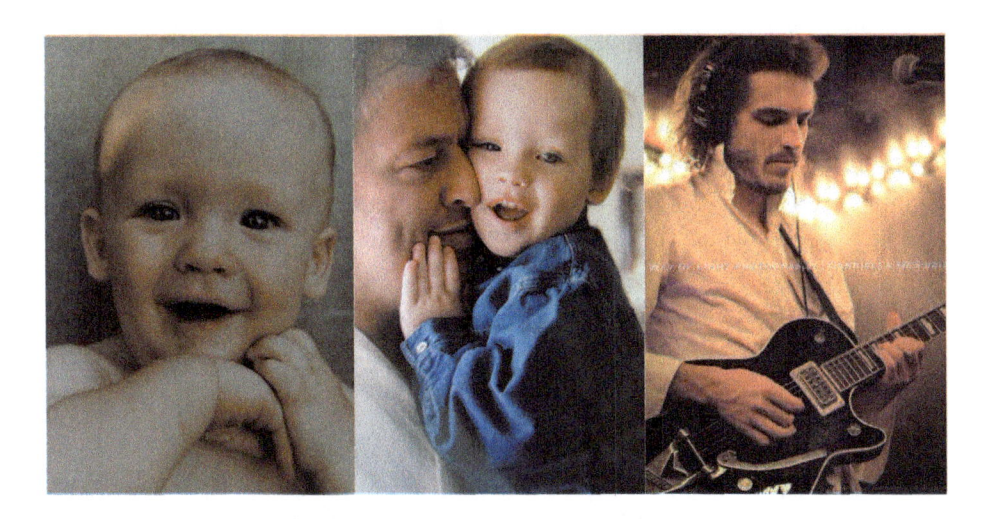

ANOTHER CHILD IS BORN AT HOME
MATTHEW GILMOUR
1985

While David was on tour I asked if he minded me going off for a few days to a peace conference in Amsterdam. The children would be fine as we had a wonderful nanny whom I trusted implicitly. Her heart was gold and she had been with us for a while. She was Annie Rowland. Bless her. Our hearts were one when it came to loving the children.

I had begun to go to meditation classes with a Sufi teacher called Mrs Irina Tweedie. She was one of the lecturers at the conference. We always had lunch in the cafeteria where the conference took place. I was in the queue and filling my tray with an array of delightful looking food when someone from the group came up to me. He said, "Mrs. Tweedie wants to see you." Not knowing what to do under these circumstances, I asked him, "Ummm, do I eat first, take my food with me or just go?" He replied, "Just go. She is waiting for you downstairs."

So I put down my tray and followed him. She was sitting in the corner wearing black, which she did when she was on duty. I came close. She said, "Sit down, dear." Nervously I did. "Ginger, I need to tell you that you are carrying a king inside you. It is a boy." I blinked and started to review when my period was due. "Don't worry, all will be well. He is a lovely soul." Well, if that wasn't a showstopper. Obviously, it was time to get a pregnancy test done.

Therefore, when I returned home, I did the test and sure enough Mrs Tweedie was right. David was home, and when I told him, he went quiet. I panicked silently. I knew he was under great stress, but the degree of which I had no idea. He had held a lot to himself as of late, but I could feel an undercurrent of tension. The whole Pink Floyd financial pressure was paramount in his mind; to what extent would not manifest until a while later.

I was focusing on my pregnancy and the kids. With each one, I developed my vision further of how special the environment was for a child when it was their moment to enter the world. This time I met Leboyer. Mrs Tweedie had us all go to a lecture he was giving in London. His vision had progressed beyond a baby being born into water. He had spent time in India with mothers who used vowels in their pregnancy and delivery. Leboyer then returned to Europe and the UK to encourage western mothers to do the same. His lecture that evening really inspired me.

We contacted each other and he referred me to a midwife who had worked and studied with him; she lived in London, and her name was Gwen. Her surname has left my memory. We met regularly and practised the vowels "A" (Ah) and "O" (Oh). Since I'd had the last two births at home this would be no problem to do again; the NHS would agree. Since my first pregnancy, Spiritual Midwifery inspired me. My ultimate dream was to give birth on the floor. So this would be the one, as I had no other physical complications and Gwen was on the same page.

I meditated each day and sang to the baby growing inside me. I continued going to Cecil's classes while I still could. One day while we were working with colour in the summer, Cecil came up to me and said, "Did you know your baby is wearing a crown?" Again, a sign from above as to what the baby's nature was. Another indication surfaced when I was driving to London from our old house to the new one. I had experiences of my baby radiating a meditative energy. I was on the motorway driving 70 miles per hour when I had to do some serious talking to him. Normally my meditative energy came from the crown or the heart centre. This time it was coming from my tummy and it was so powerful. I nearly had to stop. Meditation is not normally something one did while driving on the motorway. Fortunately, I managed to get it under control. When we eventually moved into London, and as I got larger, someone from Mrs. Tweedie's group would pick me up in their car. It meant a lot that I could get there and be in her energy. I wanted our child to grow in Peace. I was too big to drive at that stage. In fact, it was a daily feat to climb the stairs of our London home in my last few weeks. I did have to laugh as I waddled around the house and struggled up the long flight of stairs. I could have done with a chair lift. Towards the end, I had to plan my day for which room I would stay in. I read a lot.

On 24th October 1985, I went into labour in the late evening. And on the 25th, Matthew Jon Gilmour came into the world. We had placed a mattress on the floor at the bottom of our bed. He came quickly. And the vowels were incredible! Gwen did not have to ask me, "Are you in pain? Are you having contractions?" For when I was having them, I would sound either the "Ah" or the "Oh." She would know the length and the frequency, AND she would know if I was not in control for another vowel would appear: "EEEEE." I would go into shallow breathing. It was important to breathe into my womb with an open "Ah" for it kept the passageway open for the baby to come easier. An "EEEE" meant I was tense and panicking. Whenever this happened, Gwen would sound the vowels from a peaceful place to re-align me. It was amazing! Such group work.

We all slept together, David, the baby and I. We slept together for months as we had with our other babies. I stayed at home for nearly a month this time. I had come to realise that this was as important for me as for the baby. I wanted us to bond together before entering the outside world. No loud noise for us this time and no going out into the shops either until we were ready.

Each pregnancy was different, and I learned so much, especially about myself. I often wondered why it was that when one became more a master in creating sacred moments in childbirth that one could no longer go on having babies. Nevertheless, this too was to change, for the opportunity arose several times to work with couples throughout their pregnancy in the years to follow.

The day came to decide upon a name for the baby. David and I always had a list of names that we agreed upon, but Alice had it in her mind that Matthew had to be a John. Olivia Harrison called one day and Alice answered. David was not home, and Olivia respected the need for quiet time for mom and baby. So she asked Alice what we had chosen to name our baby. Alice said, "John."

A while later, the Harrisons sent us a gift to honour his birth with an engraved silver egg cup and spoon. It said 'John Gilmour'. OOPS. Alice was not too happy when we said he was to be named Matthew. She was so sad that we came up with a solution. We called him Matthew Jon Gilmour. They call him Matt now and he has become a musician and songwriter in his own right.

MOMENTARY LAPSE OF REASON
DARING TO BE
1985–1989

Day after day, the sting got stronger. Accusations came from all directions. The battle for the name went on and on. I remember the moment David further closed his heart, and rage took its place. He tried to contain it, isolating me from the process. However, the wall of protection and readiness for battle came between us as well. I remember thinking, if this is what it takes, then go for it! His integrity, his rights, his principles were at stake. I silently stood beside him before the wall. A battle cry went out. 'Pink Floyd' is ALIVE! His mind left Gilmourland, as his focus changed, directed toward the attacks. He was determined not to lose. Nick joined him, and so did Rick.

They questioned, "Can we do it?" The nerves were high. The gauntlet was mainly held by David, as the creation of the next album developed. The fire inside had grown dim, but rose again from his anger within. In a creative process, David was by his nature a person who sought to work together with everyone involved, even to compromise to get the album done. However, if injured and walked over, he stands immovably stubborn. In this instance, the pain was intense and I watched each of the band members rage in theirs. David hurt, Nick hurt, Roger hurt, Rick was no longer there and Steve held the reins tightly. The press had a field day as their fans teetered in their opinions.

I watched and continued to hold the routine at home with the kids, my heart left alone in the task. His alienation was greeted with love and support, as I knew this was bigger than we were. He stood for equality, respect and justice. The voice of justice would soon be heard and clear the way. Days in court pursued them—solicitors after solicitors—and in the end they won. It did not tear down the inner wall because there was more to carry, as we went into our future. Roger screamed, "They are a spent force!" "No way!" they shouted to the world. Determined, they went forth holding the vision. Bob Ezrin stood by them after what had transpired.

The Pink Floyd name was theirs. It was time to make an album. They knew they had to get it right. Otherwise, they would be slaughtered. It was a 'very careful' album, well done but careful. David and Nick felt touring to be an integral part of being in a band. However, despite winning the lawsuit, the record company still stood on pins and needles. "Which one's Pink?"

In that climate, finding a promoter that would take a risk was a challenge. Was Pink Floyd just a shadow of what went before? Roger's voice went far, heralding his bitter attacks that he was the one, "They won't do it!" "YOU WILL NEVER DO IT!" That was just the thing needed to strengthen David and Nick's resolve.

Eventually, they found a promoter that dared to do it in Canada. Michael Cohl saved the day. Not knowing if Roger would issue an injunction or not, he began to sell tickets. They sold out quickly. But there still remained the question of how the fans would receive Roger not being there. On top of this was the question of how they would pay for the setup.

I stood within this force, on high alert and concerned. Little did I know that David had mortgaged our home and Nick sold his 1962 GTO Ferrari for $14 million to finance the venture. I sensed some- thing extra was happening that was worrying in my heart within the tension. We, our family security, were on the tightrope as well. Millions were needed and found. I wish he had shared it with me. He would have known how much

I supported him all the way. I trusted him. No wonder David grew more withdrawn from me. Our eyes stopped meeting. I kept looking. He was holding more than tension. He was holding a secret.

Then one day Steve O'Rourke took me out for dinner, alone, in our little quaint restaurant down the road. From behind his glasses, his jaw terse, he delivered the message that the band would have to do another tax exile. I stared through him, as I remembered David's words after the last one, "Never again." However, again had just arrived and Steve was instructed to tell me. I wondered why. My heart ached in quiet desperation. Was I becoming more English? I continued yearning for our love to return. Each night as I held the children in my arms, tears would often escape, revealing the truth of my inner dilemma. The emotion arose within me in the night. I struggled to hold a positive outlook for our future.

Back in Gilmourland, preparations continued to travel again after our summer in Lindos. We were to start in Toronto, Canada. The band would be rehearsing for four weeks in a bonded warehouse at Lester Pearson International Airport. They had created a huge spectacle 'à la Floyd,' but a lot had changed technically since they had last been on the road. Rehearsals were imperative. Timing was imperative. Instead of a handful of technicians, there were 200. I lost track of all their names as they came and went. Faces would begin to be familiar and then disappear.

There were three separate stages that required manoeuvring across continents in the year to come. The technical side was more complicated than ever before. The mixing area looked like NASA base control. Before, when I sat there it was so much tinier. Now, I felt as if I was in a spaceship listening to ground control. In addition, the loading of the trucks had become a science. What a task it was to load and unload the trucks—it was larger than the *Animals* tour! Trucks to take away. Trucks to unload in relay.

I remember how small our little ones were when they stood before the eighty-foot-high stage in the echo of the warehouse, their little blonde heads leaning backwards as they looked for their dad. It was HUGE! A metal cage one hundred and sixty feet long and ninety feet deep was created, almost the size of a Boeing 727. The warehouse was a perfect place to rehearse for the tour. It was private and secure, with lots of space to play and build.

Eventually word got out. Small groups of people passing by would stop and listen. On the night of the full run-through, they had an audience. The hangar doors were open to let the summer breeze cool the air as the rumble of the aeroplanes taxiing added to the sound effects. It was an unplanned, spontaneous gig as slowly the hangar was filled inside and out by airport personnel. In addition, a collection of service and emergency vehicles congregated, with swirling lights, around the doorway. From a distance, the light show seeped out of the cracks of the warehouse making it look like something out of *ET* or *Batteries Not Included*.

We were renting a wonderful home on Lake Ontario. Each evening the children and I would walk to the edge, climb down to the jetty with bread and feed the birds. The lake spread out before us for miles, empty. The blues and pinks of the approaching sunset filled the sky. It was quite breathtaking. The girls were excited, waiting for the moment to arrive each evening. Matthew was a babe in arms, a toddler. "Mommy, Mommy, where are the birds?" "Just wait, they will come. Start with little pieces and drop them into the water." One by one, from out of the blue, birds would start to fly towards us; so many that on some days we did not have enough bread.

HARMONY OUT OF CHAOS
New York City
5–7 OCTOBER
1987

The Floyd were playing Madison Square Garden over three consecutive days. *Momentary Lapse of Reason* had been on the road and it was the first concert in the city without Roger. The gigs before proved that the band was still in business. 'The Floyd is still ALIVE' was the word on the street and the headlines throughout the press. Chinese whispers spread from state to state. The magic was still there. They had succeeded, but there was still work to do to rebuild the walls.

Before we left England, Mrs Tweedie, my meditation teacher, had asked me if I could take the draft of her book to Dr. Werner Engel, the president of New York's Jungian Society. He was to write the foreword and I would be there to ensure he got it. Once we settled, I called him, and a deep Germanic voice answered, "Yes? Engel here." My shyness kicked in with the realisation that I was about to speak to someone who was a highly regarded Jungian. I found my voice and told him why I was calling. We arranged to meet the following morning at 11am.

He had an apartment very close to where John Lennon had lived. I rang the bell and was let in by a woman who ushered me to sit in one of the multiple chairs in the long corridor. The walls were lined with certificates, framed pictures, bookshelves filled with books, and tables. I waited patiently until he finally came. His deportment was gentle and gracious as he invited me to come into the next room from whence he had come.

The room was like entering into a Victorian film set: books piled high on every table, aspidistra on a pedestal in the corner, dim light entering the room through the lace curtains. He offered me to sit in a leather chair next to his desk, which was covered with piles of papers. He pushed them aside, looking for pen and paper. I handed him the manuscript. Looking through his eye glass he said, "Well Ginger, what brings you to New York?" His demeanour was so clear and full of genuine interest, a quality I found easy to trust. His compassion opened my heart. It felt as if he was speaking directly to my soul. I lost all perception of the time as we chatted and had tea.

At one point he asked, "Ginger, I am very interested in how rock 'n' roll music affects the psyche. I was wondering if there was any way you could help me in my research?" With a rather girlish grin, cocking my head, I said, "I think that would be possible, Dr. Engel. When are you available?" We arranged for this to happen a few days later, but in the meantime, he invited me to come again the next day for he said that he would like to talk to me more about Mrs Tweedie's book.

On the designated day we organised a limousine to pick him up early, at his request, for he wanted to see everything. I met him as his car arrived with all his passes. I gave him the grand tour, for we had enough time. He questioned everyone about the technical aspects and then more psychological ones regarding life on the road. I took him to his seat as the audience was coming in. I asked if he would like earplugs but he said, "No. I want to experience the whole show." He was eighty-six. Afterwards I took him backstage to meet the band. While having a drink and a nibble, he said to me, "Ginger, I do not know if you will agree with me, but the place where you and I touch through meditation, is the same place your husband's group reaches while transforming chaos into beauty."

His words captured so much. Over the years, this always touched my heart. The flavour of Beauty that remained after all the pain. I had come to realise that the task of life was to transform chaos into Beauty. This is what our love meant to me. Despite the challenges, we have always allowed Beauty to win. This is what, even today, I feel; David's emphasis on the importance of what the underlying music spoke was essential. It sought to uplift, not to drag down, to break-through not to break-down.

Nick quoted in his book *Inside Out*: "The thing to do is to really move people; to turn them on; to subject them to a fantastic experience; to do something that stretches their imagination." I want to add: it was the music's transforming quality of the "Darkness," which spoke to us all. It reached beyond the words to our hearts in the notes they played. It silently, in its Beauty, gave us hope in a troubled world. I have said thank you so many times upon reflection, for the inspiration that gave me courage to create Beauty at all costs. Losing that quality brings our demise. This I gained without knowing about it. It was a seed planted that would grow to flower later.

WEMBLEY CONCERT
AUGUST 1988

The band toured throughout Europe and were home the first few weeks in August, before going back to America on the northern leg of the *Momentary Lapse of Reason* tour. They had two gigs scheduled on Friday the 5th and Saturday August 6th at Wembley Stadium. As I recall, Sue Turner, our secretary, and I had our work cut out for us, managing over 1000 tickets just for our friends and family, not to mention backstage passes. On top of which, Mrs Tweedie was interested in coming. This phase of touring with the Floyd was not only the congregation of family, film stars and known musicians as before, but also philosophers and spiritual leaders of the times.

The seating plan was always one of balancing who sat next to whom. The mixture of many groups of people, estranged and friendly, and cultures was a test; and yet harmony seemed always to be there in their differences. Art had a way of doing that, especially in my experiences with the Floyd. Or perhaps it was our mutual philosophy of care for the ones we loved and respected. The gig went very smoothly and Mrs Tweedie found it an interesting experience. She, like Dr. Engel, wanted to know what influenced the younger generation's psyche, first hand. She even went so far, one year, as to take an acid trip with Timothy Leary in California.

After such a large organisational feat, I had always felt it was important to honour my closest staff for working beyond the call of duty. In this case, it was Sue Turner. Burning the midnight oil upstairs in our little office at EMKA, the Floyd's offices, was often where she could be found. This year I wanted to do something EXTRA-ordinary for her. I pondered it for a few days. The touring pace continued on to Manchester and Dublin. She had been on duty each day, often with little rest.

I stayed home with the children. Then it came to me. I would send her a dozen roses every hour throughout the day, starting at 9am until 5pm. Her day usually finished between 5.30 and 6pm. After the fourth delivery, Sue was pleading with the driver, "Please tell me, are there any more coming?" He said, filling her arms with the next bunch of flowers, "No idea, luv." I asked the florist to keep it a secret. When the day drew to a close, Sue went home in a London black cab full of roses, smiling.

DADDY TOO LOUD
JAPAN
1988

David had been away for two months touring in Australia and New Zealand. I was to join him in Japan with Matthew, who was just about three. The girls had to stay back in the UK as they were still in school. English schools were getting less sympathetic about us taking them out on tour or to other exotic places except in the holidays. I loved watching David together with Matthew. They were like carbon copies, little and larger. They were mates. David always wore a brown leather flying jacket and so did Matthew, for I had found a child version in one of the London markets.

Some of the first concerts were to be in Tokyo. Matthew was always attracted to David when he sat at home or backstage or in the hotel playing the guitar. He would teeter on the edge where David was sitting, listening, fascinated. The day came when I said that we would go to the concert and hear Daddy playing on stage. We went together for the rehearsal, including our nanny, Rebecca, intending to stay through the evening concert. I took Matthew out to the mixing desk to let him get around in freedom. He loved running around the empty seats. The auditoriums were like being in a huge playground, except for the wires. Thank God, the wires were taped down. All the roadies loved our kids. They were big brothers and the kids had a very large family.

The rehearsal was about to begin so I walked over to where Matthew was playing. "Matthew, Daddy is going to play now. We must go and be at the mixer." I held him, jumping about with childlike enthusiasm, in my arms as we wandered over to where we could stand. For a moment, his eyes were at attention looking everywhere at what seemed like the starship Enterprise. He was fascinated with all the little flashing lights on the mixers and men with headsets calling cues. He always observed the little things.

Sounds of roadies clattered as the band entered onto the stage. David picked up his guitar as the rest of the band took their places. With the first note that loudly travelled around the empty auditorium, Matthew screamed, "DADDY LOUD! DADDY LOUD!" His shouting continued as I hurriedly took him down the aisles to the safety of the backstage. The music got louder as we sought refuge. The band went into full swing. The auditorium was pulsating with the volume. His little hands clung to his ears as he continued to shout, "DADDY LOUD! DADDY LOUD!"

My pace got faster, all the while wishing I had ear protectors for my child. It was not quite what I had expected. The other children had seemed ok in the past. Matthew was a sensitive child to loud sounds at home; I should have thought ahead.

All was good throughout the rest of the day. He played backstage, eating the meal I had packed for his dinner and the snacks, I might add, provided for the band. He played with many who thought he was cute. Eventually, he fell asleep on the comfy couch in the dressing room until it was over, when we could take him back to the hotel. Another day on the road with children had drawn to a close.

DAVID LEAVES THE FAMILY
WHERE IS DADDY?
COMFORTABLY NUMB

David was still on the *Momentary Lapse of Reason* tour so I took all of the children to Lindos. We decided to stay at our home in Pefkos to be more with nature. Each evening we would come back from the beach, shower and watch the sunset. The eucalyptus and pine trees would impart their fragrance as the evening cicadas sang, announcing the approaching night. We loved our miniature Italian Rhodian Villa, built in the twenties.

David eventually arrived and we were all happy to have him back with us. He looked tired. The stress was showing from him having taken on the main responsibility for the band on this last phase. He would stay out late. To some extent, I knew that this would be the case. Coming home off a tour of gigs and late nights does not make it easy to step back into home life. But my heart really yearned for him to be back. It yearned for the David I loved.

One night David had gone into town and I was to meet him after I put the children to bed. A knock came at the front door. It was Sue Turner, our previous nanny, now secretary. It was nightfall and she had flown in with some urgent papers for David to sign. She left as suddenly as she arrived, to catch David in town. At the time, I was in the dark. But for sure, it had something to do with work. Later I was to discover that it pertained to the record company wanting another album. She had brought the contract to sign. Our life was still being determined by the needs of owning the Pink Floyd name, and (I believe) our not-so-sure financial situation.

The next morning, while we were having tea on the veranda, with Matthew sitting on his lap, David told us that he needed more time to unwind. He therefore would not be coming back to the UK with us. The children had to start school so there was no way for us to extend our stay. He had promised that we would start to have more time together, but he really needed to have some time out. I could sense that there was more weighing on his mind. His silent repose was his pattern even though words of concern showed in his eyes. I had learned to wait, to get on with daily matters and keep praying for the best.

David returned home, but instead of fulfilling his promise to be with us, he had to go back into the studio. He would work late into the night. Our home life filled with broken promises to have dinner with us time and time again. I asked him if he was to be late, please just call and tell me. He said yes but didn't. He promised to take the children to school, but couldn't get up. I covered for him with more stories. They listened with a pout. He was not there. What had once been Roger's story was now ours. There was no one home in his being. It seeped in and suddenly there it was. I had no idea which way to turn. The coldness went deep. Caught in the briar sang in my heart. Stuck between the thorns. What happened to the joy, the love?

Not knowing when David would arrive home repeated itself again and again. I had no idea what to expect next. This was not the David I knew. When on another night he did not come home at all, I could not sleep as the hours went by with no word. He was not at the studio. He had already left. I called Steve O'Rourke. He had no idea where he was.

I was fraught with worry. In the morning the children asked, "Where is Daddy?" I lied and said that he had to work late at the studio. After the school run, I called the studio. Phil Taylor was there and said that they expected David around 11am. Something inside me broke. No more stories. No more lies. No more waiting. I exploded. I packed a suitcase and drove to the studio. He was there. "Where have you been?" I shouted, holding my tears. No answer. Our eyes stared into the space between us. He was 'Comfortably Numb'. The song had become the man. "You promised! I cannot cover you anymore with the children. I need YOU!" I dropped the suitcase before him and said, "Come back when you are ready to be with US!" He never came back.

We did have a chat with the children about the state of affairs weeks later, but they continued to hope he would come back. Months went by and then he sent Jerome with some separation papers for me to sign. From time to time David did come to see the children and get more belongings. One day when he came, I was writing at our desk upstairs. The door was open. I could feel him standing there held in silent desperation, watching, searching for something to say. I did not turn to draw out his thoughts as I did in the past. I waited, but he left. I really don't remember much of that period. My mind was empty. My heart hurt. It is all a blur. One thing is for sure: I was amazed how much room in my mind was a vacant space, once filled with thinking every day as a wife and mother.

Our house, Monksbridge, overlooked the River Thames. We had a huge chitalpa tree with a wooden swing. In those days, I would swing in quiet reflection while the children were at school. Sometimes, I would wander and sit by the river. There was a little island with a bridge, which led to another part of the garden closer to the river. It is said that King Edward and Lady Simpson used to stay at Monksbridge. In fact, they gifted the property with a teddy bear shaped topiary tree as a present, which someone planted on the island. Most days I would go over the bridge and sit. I would watch the leaves pass by in the current moving downstream.

One day when I was sitting there with such remorse, I was not sure whether there was any life for me after David Gilmour. I contemplated ending it. I saw through my grief, to the place where I was free. I had seen this place before as a teenager. I just had to let go. Just jump. The current would do the rest. But just when it was almost a reality, I heard the laughter of my children in the garden. They were home from school. I went into automatic pilot and picked up my battered body, for that is what it felt like. Crossing the bridge, I entered into my future as a single mother with four lovely children. Little did they know that they saved their mom that day with the sound of their joy.

I shared my story and thoughts with Dr. Barot, who had become our homeopath after the passing over of Dr. Sharma. He gave me a bottle of remedies and said, "If you find yourself in that situation again, take two of these pills and wait ten minutes before jumping, if you can." I never used them. The children were my panacea. Mothering was my strength.

Their laughter helped me to remember how to laugh for my joy was clogged up.

I have since discovered the healing power of joy and laughter. It's a gift from God. I now know, from my own experience. Laughter breaks down the walls of sadness. It strengthens our immune system, clears the brain, and reduces our blood pressure, but most of all it brings healing. Since, I try very consciously not to let my laughter get rusty. Giggles keep me going.

HOUSE OF BROKEN DREAMS
KUAUI, HAWAII
1989

As I write each morning, the chapters between the threads of our marriage get longer and longer, thinner and thinner; I enter into those moments when our dreams are being broken. I have to face the emerging sorrow of the chasm that was building between us. I struggle to face the computer, to touch the keys. I ask God to please give me the strength to transform what is still held inside. I pray for help, so that joy will return and the peace of "who I truly AM" will be restored to me.

We, David and I, were living in separate houses, separate lives joined only by our children and a piece of paper affirming "until death do us part." Could we go on? We decided to meet in Kauai for a try. We never really discussed our intention; we were not really discussing much on deeper levels for years, nor did we allow our hearts to be open as before. The mask had become our relationship. False smiles, without the sparkle in our eyes, hiding the struggle, still doing the dishes and taking out the trash. The wall was being built with each day. What do we do? What can we do silently? Is it over?

The children and I travelled separately, for David was touring somewhere in the world. As soon as our feet touched the ground of Kauai and we knew our journey was over, the bliss of the flowers and the Aloha spirit of the island once again took me over. We had rented a most wonderful home. Well, it was more than a home, it was the historic plantation estate of Albert Spencer Wilcox, Keolani, which had stood for over a hundred years. In Europe, this was young, but in Hawaii, it was ancient, when you consider the weather it has probably endured. Its beauty soothed our weary hearts as we sat on the veranda looking over the lawn past the coconut trees to the blue of the ocean.

When David arrived, the children rejoiced and ran into his arms, "Daddy, Daddy!" He smiled, stooping down to hold them, looking up at me, his eyes distant, questioning, unsure. We slept in different bedrooms joined by a glass partition. And our days went on, "as if" we were a family. The children played happily as though the dream was still playing, rejoicing in the presence of their mom and dad together.

We made new friends and were truly happy that Suzanne and Graham Nash were staying on the island as well. Graham must have been an early riser. Each morning as we walked out onto the veranda by the kitchen with our tea, there was a basket laden with fresh papayas from them. I discovered many years later that David always answered the phone saying, "House of broken dreams." I am glad I had not heard him saying that, as it would have upset me deeply because I was still trying to glue the dream together. At some point, Graham asked if he could use the line for a new song. As the years go by, I still weep each time I hear it. So beautiful, but so sad.

After this time together it was evident our family was to split into who had the kids on which weekend. David continued touring and I continued with my Jungian analysis with Hella Adler in Burgess Hill, now that Dr. Adler had passed. She had completed her religious observance to the Judaic tradition that they both shared in these matters. She was ready for us to begin. Her consulting room was upstairs, full of sunshine. As one entered she would be sitting in a large comfy chair right there before you, her knees covered with a blanket and a gentle smile of welcome. As with Gerhard, I felt at ease in her presence. I often sat either on the couch, where there was a sheet of newspaper to put one's feet, or on a therapeutic rocking stool placed nearby.

Working with her gave me hope that I could go further along my inner journey that my soul longed for and that she would be my companion along the way. Mrs. Adler often worked with me through creative drawing with my imagination. The most revealing one was an individual slumped on the floor in the shadow against a wall. She was held confined in a small room with no door. High up on the wall, out of reach, was a tiny window with a most beautiful view of the countryside. Interestingly, the shape of the individual slumped on the floor was pink, faceless and looked like the

Floyd's Pink from Gerald Scarfe's drawings for *The Wall* film. So I wonder, even today, who was I really drawing, or what part Pink had become me at the time. This image I have used for the cover of this book *Behind the Wall*.

At some point, Mrs. Adler suggested that David and I had a joint session. She asked him what he felt was the difficulty in our relationship. He responded that it was Mrs Tweedie. She asked why he felt that way. He said, "She is power mad and controlled her followers." She furthered by asking him, "Do you think that Ginger is under her power?" He said, "No." She asked in response, "David, have you ever considered that both Mrs Tweedie and Cecil Collins were giving her a more positive mother and father presence to heal her childhood experiences?" He was silent. We left Burgess Hill that day in separate cars, separate houses, separate lives.

ISLE OF DOGS CONCERT
JULY 1989

The *Momentary Lapse of Reason* tour had returned from Paris to play for six nights at the London Arena in the Isle of Dogs, London. The children were going and suggested that I should as well. I tried to resist their pleas for the pain was too close. Alice, bless her heart, said that I MUST and went about organising my tickets. She had difficulty and was embarrassed to tell me that the only tickets I could have were in the bleachers, not with them. I decided to brave the storm to honour Alice's efforts.

And a storm it turned out to be, but more for the audience. For some bizarre reason, the London authorities requested the fans to enter the arena in single file. The Floyd were known to be punctual, but this night it was broken. It couldn't be. What should have been a 7.30pm start became an 8.10pm start. To make matters worse, the beginning of the show was further broken as many entered late. The laser beams cutting across their vision and smoke from above made it more difficult as they clambered for their seats.

It was such a commotion. Balancing their drinks and food, many already seated had to stand while others settled. It created quite an unexpected disturbance as we tried to be held by the music.

The problem that helped create this clamour lay in the fact that once inside the first doors, there was a special offer:

Special offer: 5oz hamburger, relish and lager £3

The Brits love their lager at a concert. I always found this to be in sharp contrast to other countries, the allowing of alcohol at a show. Consequently, there were long queues of fans, already late, buying hamburgers, lagers and T-shirts. And I was amongst them, not buying, but just getting in along with the other ticket holders. I had rented a limousine and Hank was our driver. Jill and Andy Robson and a friend came with me. It was a bizarre beginning as our limo left us out in front of the arena. Hank, who I knew well from our tours, would wait until it was all over in the main parking lot. He said, "Call me when you want to leave."

Our seats were on the side bleachers as Alice said they would be. My breathing was a bit short as my anxiety built waiting for some fear to go away, some embarrassment to fade and carry my heart pain. There were sounds of an aeroplane going overhead that got the audience shouting and excited, but it was not part of the show. It was a plane going to land at Heathrow Airport. Good timing—it fit right in, and memories of the American *Animals* tour returned. The show began. David entered on the stage and gave a run-down of what to expect.

My heart stopped as I sat far away in the shadow. Song after song played. The fear changed to an inner smile because I was listening to part of my life story. I heard the joy and the love that had been there. With each song another memory returned. Where I thought hearing the music would stir the wound, it didn't. I was filled with gratitude for my life instead. I no longer had to run away when I heard the songs playing in the shops or restaurants. I was happy to be me. That evening helped to wash and temper the pain.

LOVE, LOSS & WONDER

Before I close my story of my journey of 'Love, Loss & Wonder' further, I felt it important to share an insight I had during this time. Ever since I was little, there has been a flavour, a fragrance of energy, which has always guided me. Sometimes it has been full of grace, other times a warning just before I touched the electric barbed wire fence.

Fortunately, despite many challenges along the way, I feel, it mainly has been full of grace, for which I am eternally grateful. Step by step, it has come closer and closer, this fragrance. Many methods, many teachings have guided me until this very moment. Today, a new awakening is guiding me. After many years of searching, the cherry is being placed upon the cake.

Around the time that my mother was passing over and other private matters were full on, I had a vision of the Christ coming to me. This was a new experience. I had heard of many who spoke of the appearance of Christ, but was suspicious. I wanted truth, not illusions. Consequently, I found myself along a different path to God than the religion in which I had been baptised. My family and I were in Florida during my mother's last days. I held the torch for many but in my bedroom, I cried. It was a tense time, the depth of which I held to myself, always smiling, consoling, listening to others, responding, guiding. Then one night Christ appeared in my bedroom at the foot of my bed. It was so real, beyond doubt. He spoke to me so softly, full of heart, "Ginger, I have a message from God for you. He says not to worry that it has to be this way for his divine plan to work out for you, your children and your family."

The next morning, I felt differently, full of inner trust and joy. Had I found my way back to Christ? The days continued full of things to do and decide. My mother was in her final days with us. While she was still clear, she spoke to me. We were alone. Her voice changed, as though speaking from some inner place beyond the room: "Charlie, I need to tell you something. Please sit down. I have a secret I have often wanted to share with you but didn't." Gosh, I thought to myself, what skeleton is about to be revealed to me as I sat on the bed? The story of Stephen having a different father had been enough within our family dynamics many years ago. She continued, "It's been very difficult being your mother." Gulp. The air in the room grew silent and suddenly filled with light, as I waited for the story to continue.

Her black eyes sparkled as she shifted her weight, leaning upon her pillows. "Charlie, you are an Angel! A real Angel! And I didn't know how to raise an Angel. There weren't any books to help me. I couldn't tell anybody either. I didn't know why God had given me an Angel to care for as I didn't feel worthy." I was amazed at the story she shared. I reflected upon the moment that Elizabeth Collins stood at the top of her stairs. Her last words to me that day were "Ginger, don't forget your angels!" Since that day, I painted Angels. I believed in Angels. I spent years hoping to see an Angel. But to BE an Angel?

I sat on the edge of her bed, mesmerised, as she continued, "I just wanted you to know this and perhaps you would forgive me." "What is there to forgive, Mom?" I asked. A tear dropped from her eye as she said, "I might have been too hard on you, trying to protect you. And I could not treat you any different than your brothers and sisters." Her breath went softer, fulfilled from the release, the story told, she could now rest. I drove home in a daze. Those moments in my mother's final hours touched me deeply. My life perspective was changing, adjusting, and reviewing all that I have had as a guiding vision influencing my life.

She passed away in late October 2013. I have had more visitations from Christ full of warmth and love. I have come full circle to know what has always been in my heart is Him and God. Many will question this, but the reality for me is the love building in my heart. The feeling of safety grows with each day. The dream of love is manifesting beyond all I ever imagined was possible. Where I had many questions, many judgments before, I see now they were manmade pale images keeping me away from this love, which speaks louder. It always has. Goodness, Truth, Kindness, Beauty, this Wisdom were my instinctive qualities that stood within all the storms. I just didn't know the source. Who knows if I am an Angel? What I do know is that I am a human being, born to be of service.

After my mother passed, I returned to England, and I wrote this prose to honour her heart, her life and our last moments:

OUR LAST SMILE

The most intimate and transformative moment of all, was when my own mother's eyes would meet mine for the last time. Her eyes would look into my very soul and my eyes would meet her there… my smile was the last smile she saw from me, it was the last time she would reach to kiss my face, to touch it tenderly.

MY FINAL WORDS TO HER

Dearest Mom, As the sun set into the horizon
I pondered the Moment
Our souls came together as One...
You, as my Mother;
I, as your Daughter.
We have travelled many journeys
Together through this Lifetime
And perhaps many before.
Our Hearts touching
In Love & Beauty
Bringing Heaven To Earth.
I hear the Angels rejoicing
For what we have achieved
Through Life's Challenges
You, as my Guardian
My Protector in the Storm;
I as the Artist
Creator of Beauty & Kindness.
I am eternally grateful
To share the divine pathway
With YOU,
My Mother.
May peace be with you!

Most of the children were in boarding school, except for Matthew, and I no longer needed a home where children could roller skate from one end to the other. No longer did masses of their friends and parents come to make Christmas cakes for the school fair. No longer did we make the scenery together for the school plays at home on the lawn. They were on their own journey now, so I needed a place more for my own creativity to blossom. A new step was approaching. An inner call ushered forth from within my being to find a place where creativity could happen.

Throughout my life I have been graced to have met many great philosophers and teachers who have opened the doorways to my own conscious creativity. My time within the Pink Floyd gave me many moments of how creativity can induce the experience of unity and beauty amongst many. It touched the very nature of my soul, which probably allowed me to survive sometimes in very harsh conditions. Now through my teachers I have been inspired to 'Become and create Beauty' through my own innate talent as an artist.

One of my most influential thoughts, which carried me through this part of my journey, was when a friend asked if I had realised that I had the "soul of an artist." He had observed me over the last ten years and no matter what I put my hands to it was a piece of artwork.

I love this phase of my life, discovering *the soul of the artist*. Each time I went to my studio to create, even today, I am inspired by words from Cecil Collins' classes which I took for over eight years. He's quoted as saying:

"The art of the future will be to feed the interior life of the individual and will not be dominated by theory political, philosophical or spiritual. There must be in the world a revolution of human consciousness from the idea of fear and desire, victory and defeat, courage and cowardice, ownership and sharing. We need to return to the eternal values which are being human and divine."(Allitt, John Stewart, *The Magic Mirror: Thoughts and Reflections on Cecil Collins*, 2010)

That is the well of spring water, of inspiration, from which I seek to create—it is my quest, for I have come to realise that we are all creators of our stories and another chapter is just beginning for me through the 'Art of Creating Beauty.'

In closing, I would like to say thank you to David, and may his future be full of Love and Creativity.

In Beauty…
Ginger Gilmour

I have a DREAM VISION.....
And A NEW ADVENTURE is just beginnning......

In Beauty,
Ginger

Behind The Wall

Behind The Wall

Behind The Wall

Behind The Wall

Behind The Wall

Behind The Wall

Behind The Wall

Printed by BoD in Norderstedt, Germany